Traditional Boatbuilding Made Easy

a 12 foot skiff for oar and sail

Traditional Boatbuilding Made Easy

a 12 foot skiff for oar and sail

A WoodenBoat Book
by Richard Kolin

Book design by Lindy Gifford
Cover design by Richard Gorski
Peter H. Spectre, Editor
Patricia J. Lown, Proofreader

Printed in the United States of America

Cover photograph: Neil Rabinowitz

A WoodenBoat Book

ISBN 0–937822–40–X

To Cathy, Annie, Heather, and especially Heidi,
whose cheerful, upbeat smile makes us all feel good.

Acknowledgements

Many people helped me learn the trade of boatbuilding. Most were the friends, customers, students, and fellow enthusiasts who stopped by my shop to compare notes.

I owe much to Howard Chapelle, who I never met or corresponded with, but who nevertheless was a significant influence, as for many years his books were my only access to boatbuilding knowledge. I still refer to my well-worn copies of *American Small Sailing Craft*, *Boatbuilding*, and *Yacht Designing and Planning*.

I owe thanks to Bill Grunwald, in whose shop in Davenport, California, I built my first wooden boat. Bill's determined effort to keep alive the craft of wooden boat building is a legend in the central California area.

John Gardner was a major influence, both through his writings and his correspondence. He was always helpful and informative, no matter how feeble the question. I still have in my files photographs that he sent me over 20 years ago of boats built in the boatshop at Mystic Seaport. He was the force behind my becoming the founding editor of the *The Ash Breeze*, the newsletter of the Traditional Small Craft Association, an assignment that gave me the opportunity to correspond with many experts in the field, some professional, some amateur, some well known, some not.

Pete Culler was one of my early inspirations and mentors. He never failed to answer letters promptly and tolerated phone calls at odd hours. His knowledge and artistry showed what could be done in the designing and building of small wooden boats. His advice that "experience starts when you begin" helped me make the transition from being a reader to a doer. His work with what he termed "good little skiffs" influenced my own work; this influence can especially be seen in the construction plan of Heidi. Pete was the one who insisted that a good pair of oars was required for good rowing performance, and that the best oars are those you build yourself. I always pass on this indispensable advice.

I pass on all of this knowledge I learned from others and from my own experience in the hope that you will find the excitement and feeling of accomplishment that I have found. It would be only fair to all of these fine people who gave of their time and experience to help me along to say that the best of this book was influenced by them; the rest I made up myself.

So now it's your turn. Go to it and have fun!

Introduction

In my twenty-five years of boatbuilding, the skiff stands out as my favorite boat type. None other has its simplicity, elegance, and practicality. It is fast, rugged, quickly and inexpensively built, and easy to repair. In a few words, it is the ideal boat for the first-time builder.

Skiffs are sturdy and stable, and yet are remarkably fast. They are ideal for kids large and small, for fishing, rowing, and cartopping. Most of them tow well and can handle a low-power outboard, under two horsepower. They make great sailboats, too.

I have designed and built skiffs for both plywood and plank construction. Both construction types have their advantages and disadvantages, but if you want to try your hand at traditional craftsmanship, planking with sawn boards is the only way to go. Shavings of old-growth cedar, fir, and oak have that familiar feel and smell that put the craftsman in touch with his or her roots. Mastering old skills that flow with nature instead of confronting it will give you satisfaction that will last a lifetime.

There is much anxiety attached to the idea of building a traditional wooden boat, since the use of simple hand tools, once a staple of life, has become an exotic activity in our times. This has given birth to a myth that imagines that the skillful use of these tools requires a lifetime of experience and is therefore out of the reach of the average person. Nothing could be further from the truth. Tools were invented to make work easier!

The basic hand tools, such as planes, spokeshaves, and chisels, have had centuries to be perfected for effective use. Students who have attended my classes catch on to this within minutes. The key is to get the tools sharp and to learn their proper use.

The skiff Heidi was designed for a class that I taught at the Center for Wooden Boats in Seattle, Washington, in the spring of 1994. She was built by students who had never built a boat before yet did a beautiful job. Their skiff is now part of the rental fleet at the center. Heidi's construction was designed to eliminate or simplify most of the cranky elements of skiff construction, a good part of which is connected with the twist in the garboard, the lowest bottom plank, and the installation of the chine, the fore-and-aft framing member that attaches the side planking to the bottom.

A lifetime of working in and around boatyards has taught me a few tricks that I will pass on to make the job go easier. Many of these great ideas, however, were taught me by innovative students during classes. Boatbuilding is an exercise in problem solving that brings out the best in us!

This book was written to take the first-time builder step by step through the building of Heidi. It will be an adventure that will lead you to a lifetime of satisfaction. You should have a basic knowledge of tools, a few tools to start with, and a place to build.

Even if you never build another boat after this one, building Heidi will be an experience you will always remember with pride. But watch out — boatbuilding is addictive!

I

In the Beginning

Building a traditional wooden skiff — the basics

Traditional wooden boats are constructed on the principle that pieces of wood, tightly fit and well fastened, will absorb water, swell, and become watertight. Voila! No need for fiberglass, glues, and sticky goops to keep your boat from sinking.

Actually, the principle is a little more complex, as portions of the boat above the waterline dry out or absorb moisture depending on weather conditions. Some small-boat owners sometimes tie their boats to the top of the car and drive at 65 miles per hour; this will dry out the wood, which will shrink, causing the seams to open. Some compromises have to be made, therefore, for the basic principle to work.

Prior to the growth of incomes after World War II, which made boat ownership accessible, it was quite common for those who wished to use a boat to visit a boat livery (a rental business) and, for a small sum, rent a rowboat for a day of exploring or fishing. Skiffs were popular for these tasks. They were simple and sometimes quite crude. One plank per side was good enough for many, and the bottoms were made of planks four to six inches wide, either set tightly edge to edge or with a caulking seam filled with cotton and paint, and overlaid with an oil-based seam compound. The boats were usually fastened with galvanized common nails.

In the early 1950s, the livery near my house in New Jersey had boats like these simple skiffs, with no caulking seams. These boats were leaned against a fence in stacks of five or six all winter long. By springtime the seams were open a quarter of an inch. Eddy, the man who ran the place, would paint the boats with house paint, then launch them, allowing them fill with water until they were half sunk. In a week, after they were swelled up tightly, they were pumped out, ready for a summer's use. This was simple, practical, and effective.

Heidi uses many of the principles that Eddy used, but with several embellishments (Eddy's boats were not great beauties). Heidi utilizes lapstrake construction, which is light and strong, and which minimizes topside shrinking and swelling. Such construction allows us to use narrower side planks than the old single-plank skiffs, and produces a much better-looking boat. Instead of the old-style cotton caulking, paint, and seam compound, we use a rubber compound — polyurethane or a similar waterproof, exterior, flexible adhesive compound — in the seams at the transom, the lower edge of the side plank, and the stem. This modern method provides a flexible seam; our paint won't crack and the boat won't leak if the topsides should dry out.

There are two ways of building the bottom. It can be constructed of cross planking with tight seams, like Eddy's boats, or with sheet plywood, which eliminates the seams altogether. I favor the tight-seam method, as I like the idea of building my boat entirely of plank, which is more fun to work with, makes the boat more of a period piece, and will last longer, as it will take more abuse than plywood. A planked bottom, however, works best for boats left in the water. The plywood bottom is preferable for boats that will be cartopped. I will discuss both methods in detail.

What skills do I need?

Building a boat like Heidi requires a basic knowledge of hand tools: their use, and how to sharpen them. Much of this can be learned as you go. The less experience you have, the more I recommend practicing on scrap before cutting valuable wood. The boat will look better and your wallet will stay thicker. Shop floor tools like bandsaws, table saws, jointers, and planers require basic skills as well as good safety habits. For the totally uninitiated, taking an adult education course might be wise before you risk life, limb, and hard-earned cash.

What tools do I need?

The basic hand tools required to build Heidi are:

7-inch low-angle block plane
9½-inch smoothing plane
Rabbet plane
Long jointer plane
Adjustable spokeshave, one with screw adjusters
Chisel, ½ inch or ¾ inch
Assorted screwdrivers — they must fit tightly into
    the slots of the screws
File — half-round and round, medium-cut
3-inch hole saw (a power drill accessory used for
    the sailing rig)
Heavy-duty stapler
Heavy-duty scissors
Hammer
Handsaw, 10-point or equivalent Japanese pull saw
Dovetail saw, or equivalent Japanese pull saw
Pencil sharpener
1½-inch putty knife
Sharpening stones — grits 250, 600-800, 1200,
    6000-8000
Assorted clamps
    (the numbers given are the minimum)
    C clamps, six 6-inch, 4-inch
    Spring clamps, four to six 4-inch
    Pipe clamps, three (the pipes must be at least
        2½ feet long)
    Wooden cabinet or cam clamps, four 6 to 8
        inches deep, for clamping plank laps

These tools can all be obtained at considerable savings at flea markets and used-tool stores. The patterns offered by the tool manufacturers today all seem similar, whether they are bought at a fancy tool store or a lumberyard. In fact, a used tool might be much better than a new one, as many of the fine tool makers are no longer in business. Handsaws might be the exception, unless you take the extra effort to learn to sharpen them yourself. The sharpening shops today are notorious for ruining many a fine tool. A new saw will stay sharp for years with the limited use most people give them, as long as the teeth are carefully protected. If you use your saw a lot, by all means learn to sharpen it yourself.

Most old-time shipwrights have a box full of specialized planes. You won't need as many as they do, but you will need a few basic planes to get started. You can collect more if you find a need for them.

The 7-inch low-angle block plane is the workhorse of the planes, with the 9½-inch smoothing plane being the next most useful. I have seen the latter plane marketed under several labels, but most on the market today seem to have been manufactured to the same pattern. An older plane from a flea market or a used-tool store can be markedly better, so keep your eyes peeled for one. The blade adjustment on any plane, new or used, should work easily. I use a deep cut for cleaning up rough edges, then raise the edge for a smooth finish.

The bottom of this boat requires square-sided boards, which are best got out on the modern jointer, a stationary power tool. The old-style hand-powered jointer plane will produce wonderfully straight edges, but with it you can lose the square edge easily; once lost it is difficult to get back. I recommend the power jointer if you can afford it. I still occasionally use my jointer plane, which was given to me by an old boatbuilder friend. When it is quietly peeling off long curls, I remember some good times and good boats.

The rabbet plane is a specialized tool that you will need to get out the plank rabbets, also called gains, at the ends of each plank (see Figure 16 for an example). When new, this plane comes with an edge guide that greatly enhances its use. Most used rabbet planes don't have this part anymore, so I recommend buying a new one. However, an old rabbet plane can be improved by fitting a homemade edge guide or by the simple expedient of clamping a piece of wood to the plank being planed that can act as a guide.

Two sawhorses are important for this project, as they will support your boat while it is being built. The trouble with sawhorses in a small shop is they take up too much space and are therefore stored outside, where they deteriorate. One solution is to use temporary sawhorses, the parts of which are held together with clamps, but they must be sturdy enough to withstand some abuse.

I used to build permanent sawhorses, as the sawhorse clamps sold in hardware stores were flimsy. I recently saw my neighbor restoring a boat that sat on two sawhorses made with store-bought plastic clamps put together with wing nuts. I was impressed and bought a couple for myself; they work fine. Some things aren't what they used to be, and it's a good thing, too!

Sharpening stones are a must. There are many tool stores around where you can get good sharpening equipment and books describing the best ways to sharpen all kinds of hand tools. Generally speaking, Japanese water stones are the cheapest; ceramic stones might be an improvement for more money; and diamond stones last forever if you can stand the sticker shock. The old-timers didn't have any of these and relied on Arkansas oil stones and their relatives. I will talk more about sharpening in Chapter Two.

Hand power tools that are useful are:
A hand power drill with a set of twist drills and countersinks (for #8 and #12 screws)
Power screwdriver — if battery powered, it should be at least 9 volts; some also double as power drills
Finishing sander rated at 10,000 orbits
Belt sander
Sabersaw with metal-cutting blades
Panel saw — 7½-inch circular saw with a fine-tooth blade
Router with ¼- and ⅜-inch rounding bits, a ¼-inch-wide by ½-inch-deep slot cutter, and a ⅜-inch bead cutter

The hand power drill, twist drills, countersinks, and finishing sander are a must, while the rest are handy to have. The sabersaw and panel saw might substitute for much of the work done by a bandsaw and table saw, discussed later. I recommend metal-cutting blades for the sabersaw, as regular woodcutting blades only cut on one stroke and tend to tear one surface of the wood. Metal-cutting blades cut on both strokes and work great on wood.

The router will cut the slot for the spline joint used to join the planks of the transom; the beading bit will add finishing touches to the sheer plank and thwarts; and the rounding bit will knock off the hard corners.

Hard corners can be rounded over by hand, however, with a block plane and sandpaper. For that matter, beads and slots can also be hand cut with the specialized planes the old-timers used. Searching through antique shops and used tool stores might well turn up these tools, which, if sharpened well, will do the job.

Measuring tools useful for building Heidi include:
12-inch adjustable combination square
Framing square
16-foot tape measure
4-foot straightedge
Level — at least 2 feet long
Soft-lead pencils — the round type that can be sharpened with a standard pencil sharpener; do not use a square carpenter's pencil

Shop floor tools include:
Bandsaw
Table saw
Bench grinder with 60-grit wheel and possibly a 6-inch by ¾-inch hard felt honing wheel, which will leave a razor edge on tools when used with honing compound
Jointer — preferably 6-inches wide, with a long bed
Portable 12-inch planer

Shop tools cost plenty and are difficult to find used. If you have none at all and are on a tight budget, you can get most of your milling done — planing, jointing, and ripping — at a local lumberyard or boatshop. If you are working in a confined space, this could very well be the way to go as you might not have room for stationary shop tools. You can live without them!

Do I have to be a millionaire to build this boat?

That's a good question. If you add up all the items on this list and add a few I may have forgotten, you will see that only big spenders need apply. Fortunately, most people who build boats and don't have a lot of money are able to substitute ingenuity for affluence. Scrounging from relatives and friends, and shopping wisely at flea markets, garage sales, and mail-order catalogs can greatly reduce costs.

The shop floor tools such as the bandsaw and the table saw can be a hurdle. When I started my first boat repair business I bought my hardwoods from a full-service lumberyard that had a table saw, planer, and, later, a bandsaw. The gang in the yard loved to cut out my projects, compound bevels and all, and their charges were more than reasonable. Most of the fabrication I did on the docks or on the balcony of my apartment. I worked this way for several years until my business built to a point where I needed a shop. I think I actually made more money working on that balcony than paying the overhead of a shop. Yet, with the shop I could build custom boats, so the investment was worth it.

One of my mentors started his boatbuilding business by taking adult education classes. Many high school woodworking shops have tools that most boatbuilders would drool over. And they are underutilized at that!

How much space do I need?

Ideally, you should have about five feet clearance on all sides. As the boat is roughly 12 feet by 4 feet, you will require a space measuring *22 feet by 14 feet*. A one-car garage should be fine, but, as usual, builders who lack even that might find compromise to be necessary. I once built a 14-foot boat in my family room, which measured 14 feet by 19 feet. I left the shop tools in the garage. The room was heated and well lighted, and had wall-to-wall carpeting and a TV. You can build a boat anywhere!

Where can I get materials for this boat?

Once again, much is up to you. I include a short list of known suppliers in Chapter Two. Suppliers of speciality boat lumber usually have to stock high-grades of wood in what would be small lots to the usual lumber merchant, which makes for an expensive product. If price is no object, go no further; a reputable supplier of specialty boat lumber should be able to handle your requirements. But the best course of action is to scour your neighborhood for boatshops, repair yards, and lumber and tool suppliers. Seek out other home builders. Ask about what woods are available locally, who can provide milling services, and at what cost. By asking questions about the locally available woods and their usefulness for this project you will gain valuable knowledge that will help you make your purchasing choices.

I have a small stack of clear, vertical-grain fir that I selected out of the standard construction-grade lumber at local lumberyards. I have some excellent red cedar I found the same way. (I live in the Northwest, where such lumber is readily available; other just-as-suitable species may be the norm in your locality.) The quality is the same as the high-priced stock, at a fraction of the price. Ask your yard people about grades of lumber, and the advantages and disadvantages of each. Eventually you may well know more than many of the people who work in the lumberyards.

How much time do I need?

This is a tough question to answer. Everyone has their own pace, and the project shouldn't be rushed. My wildest guess is that Heidi would take the average worker about 150 hours for building and painting. If you use your garage, plan on leaving your car outside for a while. But as an old-time boatbuilder once told me: "Why in the world would a sane person park a car in their boatshop in the first place?"

Boatbuilder's jargon

If you haven't already guessed, boatbuilders have a language of their own. Let's define some of the gobbledegook.

Aft (After) —The back part of the boat.

Bevel — An angle sawn or planed onto a piece of wood.

Bow — The forward end of the boat.

Breasthook — A piece of wood cut to fit in the opening formed by the top edges of the forward ends of the sheer planks and top of the stem. It is a structural member that is key to the stiffening of the boat.

Bucking iron — A smooth, rounded piece of steel used by auto-body repairers to back up rivets and for body hammering. Boatbuilders use it to back up copper rivets and nails, and tacks. I have successfully used the head of a sledgehammer for this. (See Figure 21 for an example of a bucking iron in use.)

Chamfer — A corner of a piece of wood that has been nosed off at a 45-degree angle.

Chine — The line formed by the meeting of the side and bottom. It is also the fore-and-aft framing member that the side and the bottom are fastened to. (See Figure 1 for an exploded view of the boat's setup, including the chine.)

Clench — A process used to fasten lapstrake planking. A copper nail or tack is driven into a hole drilled through the lapped planks. Approximately one-third of the nail protrudes beyond the surface of the plank. As the nail is driven through the planks, a bucking iron is used to force the nail to bend over a small distance and then to bend the point back into the plank. The nail acts like a staple.

Fair — A line or surface that sweeps in a single direction without kinks or lumps.

Fore (Forward) — The front part of the boat.

Gain — See rabbet.

Halyard — Line used to hoist the sail.

Hardwood — Lumber cut from deciduous trees; leafed trees that shed their leaves in winter (oak, mahogany, maple, etc.).

Keel — Plank running fore-and-aft on the bottom of the boat that ties the bottom planks together and gives the boat directional stability when moving through the water.

Lapstrake — A planking method in which the lower edge of a side plank overlaps the top edge of the plank below it.

Molds — Temporary forms on which the boat is built. This boat uses three.

Planking stock — Lumber selected for light weight and strength, suitable for planking the skiff.

Post — Wood piece used to prevent the seats from sagging.

Quarter knee — A piece of wood cut to fit in the corner formed by the after end of one of the sheer planks and the transom. It is a structural member that is key to the stiffening of the boat.

Rabbet (also called the gain) — In lapstrake planking, a tapered channel cut into the forward and after edges of the side planks. It allows the lapped planks to fit flush at the transom and stem.

Rails — Hardwood guardrails at the sheer of the boat.

Rake — The tilting of the mast or other member forward or aft of vertical.

Riser — Fore-and-aft seat support on each side of the boat, attached to the frames.

Sculling — A technique by which a boat is propelled through the water with a single oar resting in a semicircular notch in the transom. The oar is held with the blade roughly in the horizontal position, and moved back and forth so the blade describes a figure eight in the water.

Sheer — Top edge of the top plank at the deck or rail.

Sheer plank — The uppermost plank to which the rail is attached.

Sheet — Line attached to the sail that adjusts the sail's angle to the wind.

Skeg — Fin attached to the after end of the bottom of the boat to give the boat directional stability.

Softwood — Lumber cut from evergreen trees, such as cedar, spruce, pine, and fir.

Spline — A piece of wood cut to fit in slots cut in the edges of two pieces of wood. The two slots and the spline form a glue joint for holding the two pieces together.

Stations —The lines on the ladder jig on which the molds are set up. The stations are obtained from the designer's drawing of the boat.

Stem — Framing member at the forward end of the boat. The forward ends of the planks are fastened to it. Heidi has an inner stem, which the planks are fastened to, and an outer stem, which is attached later to protect the plank ends.

Stern — Aftermost part of the boat where the transom is located.

Transom — Planked-up area in the stern to which the after ends of the side planks are fastened.

II

Getting Started

How to use this book

The body of this book is a complete, detailed, step-by-step guide to building the skiff Heidi. It is important that you read through each of these steps several times before you actually begin to build; these are the same steps I use when teaching students in my boatbuilding classes. As you read, review the materials list and the illustrations. Try to imagine how you will transform each piece of wood on the list into a part of the boat.

One of the pleasures of writing this book was discovering how much it was just like building a boat, but on paper. You can appreciate the same thing as you practice building your boat in your imagination; then, by the time you cut your first piece of wood, you will be thoroughly familiar with the boatbuilding process.

Preparing your shop

In Chapter One I discussed space requirements in general. Any shed the size of a one-car garage will do, but you will need more than an empty room.

First, you will need a sturdy bench with a wood vise. This can be a permanently fixed workbench or an inexpensive Stanley Workmate. Back in the days when I did a lot of work on the docks, I stumbled onto the latter tool, which is a portable, folding worktable with a clamping device built into the top that is great for clamping planks. It has storage space underneath for tools; the support bars can be used to hang clamps, ready for use. I customized my Workmate with a wooden frame for it to sit on; this frame is fitted with heavy-duty locking casters that allow the entire rig to be moved easily from place to place. (In a small shop, the more equipment on wheels, the better). The wheels also raise the table top to a working height that is better for me.

Any bench should be of a height that allows you to work without noticeably bending over. If your work bench is too low, block it up. Your back will thank you.

Get yourself several power strips — power cords with multiple outlets — and attach one to your Workmate or bench. This will limit the number of extension cords you will need. If you don't have a good system of circuit breakers, then it is best to use a power strip that includes a resettable breaker. All my power strips have this feature, and it comes in handy.

Clear and set aside a space to store your materials. Put things up on shelves if you can, as it is best to save wall space at the floor level, which is limited and usually broken up by doors, for storing the big stationary power tools, benches, and plywood if you are using it. Long planks can be stored on shelves above the doors to take advantage of the longest walls. Other lumber can be stored outside if you are not going to use it right away. I will discuss this more later in the chapter.

Have at least two sturdy sawhorses on hand. They are handy when cutting out the molds or a plywood bottom panel and a necessity for setting up the boat at a convenient working height.

Rip and plane a long batten of vertical-grain fir, approximately $\frac{5}{8}$ inch by $\frac{5}{8}$ inch. You will use this to fair up the planks and define your sheerline.

Wood

The types of wood available for boatbuilding vary depending upon your location. Hardwoods, such as oak and mahogany, tend to be more universally available, as they are commonly used in cabinet-making. Softwoods suitable for boatbuilding, such as cedar, spruce, or pine, are sometimes more difficult to find. (The sources list at the end of this chapter contains a list of lumber companies.) You should spend some time at your local suppliers, asking questions and learning what they have available. There are some general terms that are of interest to boatbuilders when they are searching for appropriate wood. Let's take a look at some of them.

Vertical grain and flat grain are terms that refer to the appearance of the grain on the flat face of the plank. Vertical grain appears as straight lines, and flat grain appears as wavy ellipses. If you look at the end of a plank, you will see that the end-grain of a vertical-grain plank is angled at 45 degrees or more (up to 90 degrees) to the flat face. The end-grain of flat-grain planks runs more or less parallel to the flat face.

These grain patterns are created at the sawmill by the way the log is sawn. A mill sawing up an entire log in a series of parallel cuts, called plain sawing — the most common method of milling logs — creates a quantity of flat-grain planks at the top and the bottom of the log, while the center section produces planks with vertical grain. More flat-grain planks are created this way than vertical grain; as a result, vertical grain sells at a premium.

Try this: Take a piece of unsplit firewood and, with your bandsaw, cut off a 2-inch-thick "cookie" from one of the ends. Study the growth rings. Now, again using the bandsaw, slice the cookie lengthwise into ½-inch-thick "planks." Note that there will be bark on both edges of each plank. Now separate out the slices from the center, those with vertical grain that is 45 degree or less. Examine the flat surfaces. Does the grain look straight? Take the pieces cut from the top and bottom of the cookie. Study the edges and the top. This is flat grain, the type of grain you are likely to see in construction-grade framing timber or pine shelving.

The sawmill can maximize the amount of vertical-grain lumber in a log by using a technique called rift sawing, or quarter sawing. This involves turning the log after each cut, so the saw is always cutting across the end-grain.

As a boatbuilder, it is important to look for vertical-grain lumber in some species. Why? Because the premium grades of lumber are usually sold clear, and some clear, plain-sawn softwood species will check or severely cup when exposed to the weather or varying degrees of temperature and moisture. Lumber from these species is best when it has been rift or quarter sawn to produce vertical grain. Nevertheless, some varieties of wood, especially those with tight knots, which tend to tie the grain together, are best when it has been plain sawn to produce flat grain.

In the Northwest, Western red cedar, Sitka spruce, and Douglas-fir are best as planking stock when they can be obtained with clear, vertical grain. Alaska yellow cedar and Port Orford cedar are best when they have been sawn with flat grain. In the East, white pine is best when it is clear, with flat grain; varieties of white cedar are best when they are plain sawn and have tight knots, which tend to reduce splitting. Obviously, care must be taken to get the right cut from each variety of tree.

Proper seasoning (drying) and storage of lumber are critical. The wide, thin planks used for planking are especially susceptible to the cupping and splitting caused by uneven swelling and shrinking when lumber is seasoned and stored for later use. Seasoning must be controlled.

Lumber, when first cut, usually contains high levels of moisture. Remember, it is the job of the trunk to pass water from the roots of the tree through the trunk to the leaves. In the first few months after the lumber is cut, this moisture will leach out of the wood and evaporate, causing shrinkage. It wouldn't do to use newly cut wood for planking, as the planks would shrink, and then cup, split, check, and twist unmercifully. Kiln drying and air drying are the two principal methods of lowering the moisture content of lumber under controlled conditions and preventing these problems from developing.

Air drying is the traditional method boatbuilders use to season lumber. The lumber is rough cut and carefully stored while it dries. The lower planks of a pile are laid on blocks, which keep them off the ground. Spaces are left between the planks and, as each layer is added, thin, narrow pieces of wood, known as stickers (the stickers I use are at least ¾ inch thick), are placed crossways at intervals between the layers to allow the circulation of air. This air circulation is vital to ensure proper evaporation of the water as it escapes from the plank. The weight of the succeeding layers keeps the planks from cupping.

Stacking for air drying is the best technique for storing wood outdoors while it seasons; it should also be used when the wood is brought into the shop so it can become adjusted to the lower moisture levels indoors. When storing lumber outside, the stacks should be covered for protection from rain, snow, direct sunlight, and high winds. Good ventilation and air flow must be maintained at all times.

The length of time that lumber requires to season or stabilize varies with the species of wood and perhaps the size of the tree it came from. A minimum of six months is about right in general, but boatbuilders have found that some species, such as Eastern white cedar, require less time.

Boatbuilders prefer air-dried lumber, as it leaves the sap and other natural materials in the wood, maintains "life," or spring, in a plank, and helps retain the wood's natural rot resistance. Air drying takes time, however, and many manufacturers of wood products need a method of drying lumber quickly and reliably. They will kiln dry the wood — stacks of green lumber are put into a special kiln for a specified length of time to drive out the moisture. There is a belief among boatbuilders and wood scientists that the kiln also drives out the properties that give the plank life; they feel the technique produces a stiff, brittle, rot-prone material — in some cases, with collapsed cells — that is unsuitable for boatbuilding.

On the other hand, a professional builder who owned a yard known nationwide for its excellence once told me that he used kiln-dried lumber in the construction of a cold-molded yacht. Experts had advised him that if the lumber was air dried to about 20 percent moisture content and then kiln dried to about 14 percent (the natural level in his area), there would be little loss of "life." I mention this as an indication that there is more than one side to the matter of kiln drying. After all, in some cases, amateur builders might not have a choice and will have to use kiln-dried lumber because this is all that is available in their area.

No matter the drying technique used, you should stay away from lumber that has been dried significantly below ambient moisture content. Much of the vertical grain fir sold in lumberyards is dried to levels approaching six percent and should not be used for planking or framing. I have used this lumber for seats, however, where stiffness is a virtue and where, because of good ventilation, rot is unlikely.

I have introduced this subject not to confuse you but to emphasize the need for you to do homework at your local boatyard, boatshop, and lumberyard. At the end of this chapter I include a list of sources of information and materials, including books and periodicals, that will help you.

For those who have learned to recognize the characteristics of good boatbuilding wood, I strongly suggest haunting the lumberyards. There are many good pieces of boat lumber that can be gleaned from the stacks of construction-grade lumber. Ask permission first and be sure to restack the piles when you have finished your search. There can be a considerable payoff if you take the time to look.

Tool sharpening

When I first started out repairing boats, finding good sharpening stones was difficult. Arkansas stones were preferred; I found mine in sports stores that sold expensive sporting knives. They are made of quarried stone and saturated with a thin honing oil, and are available in hard and soft varieties. I used the hard and somewhat coarser variety. For honing oil I used a common household oil, such as 3-in-1.

Then came the explosion of interest in the crafts and of the number of stores that specialize in fine tools. Nowadays the problem is sorting out what type of sharpening device to buy among all the choices. Two books for those who wish to learn in-depth about the critical skills required in sharpening tools are *Sharpening*, by Jim Kingshott, and *Sharpening Basics*, by Patrick Spielman; specific information about these books can be found at the end of the chapter. Read just one of them, and you will have learned almost all you need to know. I will share some of my own sharpening experience, with the provisos that my advice barely scratches the surface and that there might be some room for debate.

One summer I was at a wooden boat show giving an oar-building demonstration in a booth run by a store that sold tools. The manager looked at my scruffy old Arkansas stone and suggested that I might like using some of the Japanese water stones he was selling. He offered to give me a set if I would use them in my demonstration. I did and was so impressed that I switched. I used stones of 800-, 1200-, and 8000-grit (the lower the grit number, the coarser the stone).

Water stones are sponge-like in their ability to absorb water and are kept soaking in it. Like the oil in the Arkansas stone, the water is used to "float" the metal filings created by sharpening from the stone to prevent clogging. The 800-grit stone is used for basic grinding, while the 1,200-grit stone is used to work down the scratches left by the coarser one. For most boat work, the edge created by a 1,200-grit stone is sharp enough. But if you want a really sharp tool, use the 8,000-grit stone to remove all the small scratches and polish up the cutting edge.

Water stones are soft and lose their flatness after a short time, but they can be reflattened easily by rubbing them on 600-grit wet-or-dry sandpaper placed on the surface of a table saw or a piece of thick glass. I find that it is good to store them in a 5-gallon plastic paint can filled with water. A grating placed in the bottom of the can keeps them out of the muck that accumulates on the bottom.

I have always admired the way an accomplished wood carver can push his or her chisels through a piece or wood. A friend of mine makes beautiful carvings based on the masks and totems of the Northwest Coast Indians. In his shop he has a variety of sharpening tools. I asked him what he preferred. He told me that he hones most of his chisels on 600-grit wet-or-dry sandpaper placed on a flat, machined surface, such as a table saw. Water provides the lubricant. For honing his gouges, curved adzes, and knives, he wraps the sandpaper over an ax handle. He claims that there are many shapes in an ax handle that will conform to the edges of all of his many knives and gouges. For polishing, he tacks a piece of unfinished leather onto a board, smears some chrome polish on it (that's right — automobile chrome polish), and hones off the scratches. The edges of the tools are pulled, not pushed, over the sandpaper and leather so as not to cut those materials. I looked at the label of his can of chrome polish and found the principal component listed as jeweler's rouge. This is the same material sold by the tool stores to hone tools, for more money! Now I use chrome polish all the time.

After I started using water stones, ceramic stones came into common use. I expect they might well be an improvement. They maintain their flatness much better than the water stones but are more expensive.

What do I use now? I use diamond stones. These retain their flatness and are always fast cutting. There are at least two types that I know of — a metal plate coated with diamond grit and a plastic square covered with a thin metal honeycomb coated with diamond grit. I have the latter and like it immensely. I have stones of 250-, 600-, and 1,200-grit. The coarse 250-grit is used to regrind the angle of my blades; the finer grits are used for finishing and polishing. I use all three of these stones to sharpen my carbide-tipped router bits, too.

Beyond sharpening stones, a hard felt honing wheel, ¾ inch by 6 inches, mounted on your bench grinder, is a useful tool when a razor edge is required on your chisels. The necessary honing compounds are available at the stores that sell these wheels. It is important to read the instructions before you use a honing wheel, as misuse can lead to a nasty accident. The most important thing to remember is that while the edge of the tool being sharpened is held into the turning direction with a grinding wheel, it must be held away from the turning direction with a felt honing wheel to prevent the cutting edge of the chisel from snagging the wheel.

Let's study sharpening by considering a nice 60-year-old chisel of good construction and fine steel that you were lucky enough to find in a used-tool store for $3.00. On the down side, the wooden handle is dirty, and the blade is rusty and darkened with the grime of the ages. Furthermore, someone has apparently used this chisel as a tent peg, so the cutting edge is broken. As one old boatbuilder used to say, "It got into the hands of the ignorant!" So much the better. For very little money you will have a fine chisel and the satisfaction of having rescued it.

First, clean up the tool. Use sandpaper on the handle; a finishing sander will help here if you are careful to maintain the handle's shape. For the metal parts, 100-grit sandpaper in your finishing sander will take off the rust in short order. Do not press hard, as you will overheat the pad on your sander and melt the glue that holds the pad onto the bottom plate. Take care not to round off the corners of the blade. When you are down to bare metal, put 300-grit wet-or-dry on the sander followed quickly by 600-grit. In a matter of minutes that old rusty chisel will shine like a mirror. Now you can sharpen it up. The next steps are those you would take with any newly acquired tool.

Put the proper lubricant on your 600- to 800-grit stone (water in most cases; oil if you are using Arkansas stones). Place the chisel flat on the stone with the bevel side up. Work the chisel back and forth over the length of the stone. You may use a circular motion if you like. With all stones except the diamond stone, it is important to use the entire face of the stone to prevent uneven wear. After a few dozen strokes look at the back of the chisel. You will see the scratch marks that you have made. What you are checking for is to see if the back of the blade is flat, which is a prerequisite for successful sharpening. This step is essential even for brand-new tools, such as chisels and plane blades, as most of them are not flat.

So take a good look at those scratches. If they show that the entire edge of the tool is touching the stone — that is, sharpening scratches appear all over the back of the blade — you may continue on to the next step. If not, keep going until the blade passes this test. When the back of the blade is flat, continue on to your 1,200-grit stone, then polish it up on a 6,000- to 8,000-grit water stone, chrome polish, or some other honing device.

Once the back is flat and honed smooth, take a look at the beveled edge. If it is chipped, then you will have to grind it until the chip is gone and the edge is squared. Most people use a bench grinder for this chore, but the use of such a tool requires careful preparation and thought.

I should mention, however, that my friend the carver prefers to use a 250-grit diamond stone, rather than a bench grinder. He doesn't like what the grinder does to the temper (hardness) of his tools.

You must be careful when using a bench grinder for grinding edge tools. Most grinders turn at high speed and will overheat a blade in short order, causing it to lose its temper. To prevent this from happening, you must cool the blade by regularly dipping it in a can of water kept close by. In addition, only use 30- to 60-grit aluminum oxide wheels; higher grit wheels cut slower, causing more heat buildup. Some people like to finish off the edge with a 100-grit wheel, but I prefer to do that with a 600-grit hand sharpening stone.

A grinding wheel leaves a hollow-ground bevel, which will flatten over time as you sharpen the edge on your stones. In time, after repeated honing, the bevel will become convex and eventually will need regrinding.

Most tool stores sell adjustable sharpening guides, and newcomers as well as old-timers would do well to get one. An old-time blacksmith and toolmaker showed me how to bend a piece of metal approximately to a 45-degree angle and clamp it to a plane blade or chisel. This can be adjusted up or down the blade until the blade has the proper angle to the stone. This makes a cheap sharpening guide. If you maintain the correct angle as you sharpen, you will eliminate the need for regrinding.

What bevel should you grind on your tools? A bevel of about 25 degrees is about average for a chisel. Some craftsmen like to use a micro bevel. This means that they grind the overall bevel to as little as 20 degrees and then hone a smaller bevel on the edge at about 30 degrees. For planes, 25 degrees should do for blades that are set in the body at 45 degrees. For low-angle block planes where the blade is set in the body at 60 degrees with the bevel up, 30 degrees is about right.

Let's review the steps:

1. If the blade needs it, grind a proper bevel along the cutting edge.

2. Set the proper angle on your sharpening guide.

3. Hone first with 600- to 800-grit, then 1,200-grit.

4. Hone with a 6,000- to 8,000-grit Japanese water stone, chrome polish on an unfinished leather surface, or a strop with honing compound purchased from a fancy tool store.

Sharpening is simple and with some practice will take little time. The trick is to hone the edge regularly. The time this takes will be more than rewarded by quick, accurate, and clean cutting. And that, my friend, is the name of the game!

Materials List

Wood

Item	Dimensions	Quantity	Material
Planking	$\frac{1}{2}'' \times 8'' \times 14'$	6	Cedar, white pine, spruce
Center seat	$\frac{3}{4}'' \times 8'' \times 4'$	1	Cedar, white pine, spruce
Bow and stern seats	$\frac{1}{2}'' \times 8''$	14'	Cedar, white pine, spruce
Inner and outer stem	$1\frac{1}{2}'' \times 9''$	3'	Mahogany, oak
Transom	$\frac{13}{16}'' \times 8''$	8'	Mahogany, oak
Rails	$\frac{3}{4}'' \times 3\frac{1}{2}''$	13'	Mahogany, oak, fir
Keel	$\frac{3}{4}'' \times 3\frac{1}{2}''$	11'	Mahogany, oak, fir
Risers	$\frac{5}{8}'' \times 4''$	12'	Mahogany, oak
Frames	$\frac{3}{4}'' \times 6''$	10'	Mahogany, oak
Chines	$\frac{3}{4}'' \times 6''$	12'	Mahogany, oak
Quarter knees, Breasthook, Oarlock pads	$\frac{13}{16}'' \times 8''$	3'	Mahogany, oak
Bottom	$\frac{3}{4}'' \times 4''$	75'	Cedar, white pine, spruce
Optional bottom	$\frac{3}{8}'' \times 4' \times 8'$	1 sheet	5-ply top-quality marine plywood
Molds, braces	$\frac{1}{2}'' \times 4' \times 8'$	1 sheet	Particle board
Screw blocks	$1\frac{1}{2}'' \times 1\frac{1}{2}''$	12'	Constr. grade fir, spruce
Ladder jig	$1\frac{1}{2}'' \times 3\frac{1}{2}''$	12',12',8'	Constr. grade 2×4
Temporary backbone	$\frac{3}{4}'' \times 3\frac{1}{2}''$	11'	Pine, constr. grade fir
Oars	$1\frac{3}{4}'' \times 1\frac{3}{4}''$	(3) 8'	Spruce, fir, basswood
Batten	$\frac{5}{8}'' \times \frac{5}{8}''$	14'	Straight-grain fir or white pine

Additional Material for Sailing Rig

Mast	$2\frac{1}{2}'' \times 2\frac{1}{2}''$	11'	Spruce, fir, basswood
Sprit	$\frac{3}{4}'' \times 1\frac{1}{2}''$	11'	Fir
Partners, knees, rudder, tiller	$\frac{3}{4}'' \times 8''$	12'	Honduras mahogany, fir, $\frac{3}{4}''$ marine plywood
Daggerboard	$\frac{3}{4}'' \times 9\frac{1}{2}''$	30''	Honduras mahogany, fir, $\frac{3}{4}''$ marine plywood
Rudder (optional construction)			$\frac{3}{4}''$ marine plywood

Fasteners

Type	Size	Quantity
Copper tacks	1½″	1 lb.
#8 Wood screws, flathead (bronze, stainless)	1″	200
	1¼″	50
	1½″	50
#12 Wood screws, flathead (bronze, stainless)	2½″	20
	3″	8
Bronze ring nails for plank bottom	1½″, #12	1 lb.
	1¼″, #14	1 lb.
Drywall screws	1¼″	1 lb.
	1½″	½ lb.
	3″	1 lb.

Glue, Paint, Miscellaneous Supplies

Type	Size/Quantity	Description
Glue	8 oz. (approx.)	Epoxy or Weldwood plastic resin
Pine tar	1 pt.	For inside of bottom
Kerosene	1 pt.	For inside of bottom
Linseed oil, boiled	1 pt.	For inside of bottom
Paint	1 pt.	Enamel primer, exterior, marine grade
	1–2 qt.	Enamel finish (one or two colors), exterior, marine grade
Thinner	1 gal.	Compatible with above paint
Caulking compound	2 tubes	Polyurethane (SikaFlex, 3M 5200), polyvinyl or similar, paintable rubber compound, waterproof, exterior grade
Brushes	2	2″–2½″, 1½″ high-quality China bristles
	1	2″ China bristle for varnish
	1	3½″–4″ throwaway, for dust cleanup
Paper towels	3 rolls	For cleanup of you and your boat
Sandpaper	20 sheets	60- to 80-grit
	20 sheets	100-grit
	10 sheets	150-grit
	5 sheets	220-grit, wet-or-dry
	2 sheets	600-grit
Poster board	3 sheets	2′ × 3′ (approx.), lightweight
Gloves, dust masks, etc.		

Fittings

Item	Quantity	Description
Stem, skeg bands	6′	½″ brass, half oval
Oarlocks & sockets, bronze	1 pr. ea.	Davis type, or type that overlaps top of oarlock pad
Latigo leather	8″ × 3″	Mast collar, hole through seat
	(2) 8″ × 6″	Oar leathers
	(2) 16″ × 1″	Oar buttons

Additional Fittings for Sailing Rig

Gudgeons and pintles	2 sets	Bronze or stainless, ¾″ between straps
Small snap	1	Bronze or stainless, for rudder hold down
Medium snap	1	Bronze or stainless, attach sheet to traveler
Dacron line ¼″, 3-strand	25′	Halyard and traveler
Dacron line ⅜″, 3-strand	30′	Sheet and dock lines

Sources

Here are a few places familiar to me where you can get information and materials. This is by no means all. If you start talking to local craftspeople, you may suddenly find there are hundreds of sources.

Tools

Woodcraft (books and tools; retail stores throughout the USA; catalog available)
210 Wood County Industrial Park
PO Box 1686
Parkersburg, WV 26102–1686
1–800–225–1153

Woodworker's Supply, Inc. (tools; beading router bits; catalog available)
1108 North Glenn Road
Casper, WY 82601
1–800–645–9292

William Arden Co (discount Stanley tools; catalog available)
Woodworking
27 Stuart St.
Boston, MA 02116–4723
1–800–249–8665

Grizzly Imports (low-cost floor tools; hand tools; catalog available)
2406 Reach Rd.
Williamsport, PA 17701
1–800–523–4777

The WoodenBoat Store (tools, plans, and books; catalog available)
PO Box 78 Naskeag Rd.
Brooklin, ME 04616–9988
1–800–273–7447

The Wooden Boat Shop (tools, books, plywood; catalog available)
1007 NE Boat St.
Seattle, WA 98105
1–800–933–3600

Sails

Nathaniel Wilson
PO Box 71 Lincoln St.
East Boothbay, ME 04544
207–633–5071

Wood

Flounder Bay Boat Lumber (wood, fasteners, hardware, tools, books)
1019 Third Street
Anacortes, WA 92221
1–800–228–4691

M.L. Condon (wood)
260 Ferris Avenue
White Plains, NY 10603
914–946–411

Additional reading

Chapelle, Howard I. *Boatbuilding.* New York: W.W. Norton & Co., Inc., 1941.

Culler, R.D. *Skiffs and Schooners.* Camden, Maine: International Marine Publishing Co., 1974.

Gardner, John. *Classic Small Craft You Can Build.* Mystic, Connecticut: Mystic Seaport Museum, 1993.

Kingshott, Jim. *Sharpening, The Complete Guide.* Guild of Master Craftsman Publications, 166 High St., Lewes, E. Sussex U.K. BN7 1XU, 1994.

Spielman, Patrick. *Sharpening Basics.* New York: Sterling Publishing Co., Inc., 1991.

The Best of Fine Woodworking. *Bench Tools.* Newtown, Connecticut: Taunton Press, 1990.

Booksellers

Boating Books
International Marine Catalog
Div. of McGraw-Hill, Inc.
Blue Ridge Summit, PA 17294–0840
1–800–822–8158.

Mystic Seaport Store
75 Greenmanville Ave.
Mystic, CT 06355
1–800–331–2665

WoodenBoat Store
P.O. Box 78, Naskeag Road
Brooklin, ME 04616
1–800–273–7447

III

Setting Up

The setup is one of the most important parts of building a boat, as a bad start guarantees a poor finish. Fortunately, like most things connected with boatbuilding, the concepts are relatively simple. Having said that, I can hear the bodies hitting the floor in disbelief! As one boatyard wag put it, "Boatbuilding is one million easy-to-learn tricks. All you need is a lifetime to learn them." And so it is. But don't despair! Building this boat is the ideal way to start learning.

The only way to approach this seemingly complicated art is to break the various operations into their smallest, most simple components. Boatbuilders learn this process from the beginning, which is why the old-timers can make a complex job look so simple. If you still have doubts, never fear. We will work together on this.

Let's look at what we are about to build, review what the pieces of the setup look like, and what boatbuilders call them.

Boat jargon

Figure 1 is a visual glossary of terms we will be using. Examine it carefully for definitions of the following (the numbers correspond to those in the figure):

1. Molds at Stations 1, 2, and 3
2. Ladder jig
3. Inner stem
4. Mold screw blocks
5. Mold brace screw blocks
6. Mold braces
7. Transom brace screw blocks
8. Transom braces
9. Transom
10. Chines
11. Temporary backbone

- **Boat jargon**
- **Materials required**
- **Build the ladder jig**
- **Glue up the transom**
- **Shape the transom**
- **Cut out the molds and mold braces**
- **Cut out the inner stem**
- **Cut out the outer stem**
- **Mount the molds on the ladder jig**
- **Mount and fasten the braces**
- **Cut out the clamping blocks**
- **Cut out the temporary backbone**
- **Set up the backbone and the molds**
- **Check that the molds are vertical**
- **Check the setup**

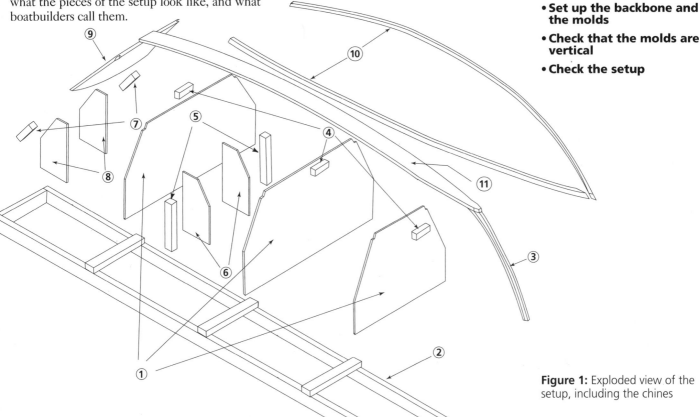

Figure 1: Exploded view of the setup, including the chines

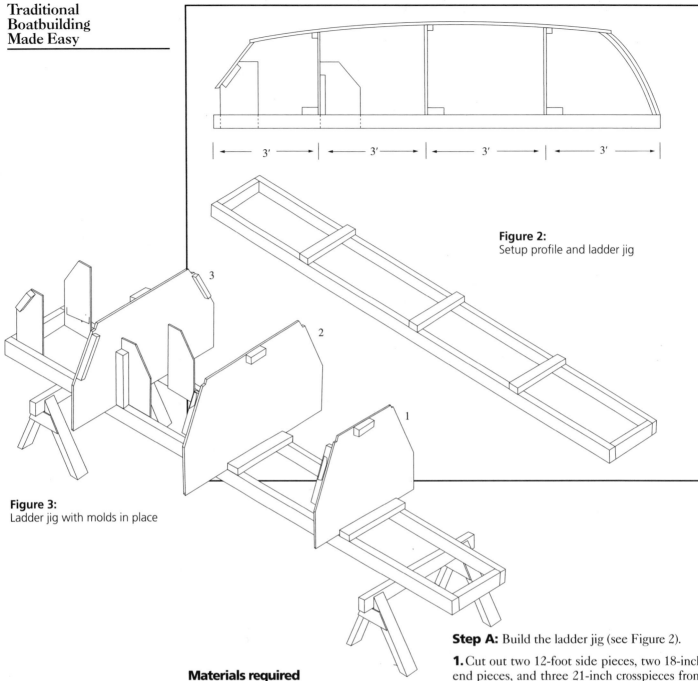

Figure 2:
Setup profile and ladder jig

Figure 3:
Ladder jig with molds in place

Materials required

Transom—two pieces mahogany, fir, or suitable substitute; each ¹³⁄₁₆ inch by 8 inches by 4 feet.

Molds, braces—one sheet particle board, ½ inch by 4 feet by 8 feet.

Screw blocks—one piece construction-grade fir, pine, or spruce, 1½ inches by 1½ inches, 12 feet long.

Ladder jig—construction grade fir, pine, or spruce, 1½ inches by 3½ inches; two pieces 12 feet long, one piece 8 feet.

Temporary backbone—one piece fir, pine, or spruce, ¾ inch by 3½ inches, 11 feet long.

Stem (inner and outer)—one piece mahogany or oak, 1½ inches by 9 inches, 3 feet long.

Drywall screws—all sizes.

Step A: Build the ladder jig (see Figure 2).

1. Cut out two 12-foot side pieces, two 18-inch end pieces, and three 21-inch crosspieces from standard 2- by 4-inch stock (actual size: 1½ inches by 3½ inches). Be sure that all pieces are straight and that the ends are square.

2. Mark station lines every 3 feet on the 12-foot pieces.

3. Using 3-inch drywall screws, fasten the end and crosspieces to the 12-foot side pieces, using care to place the crosspieces on the proper side of the station lines (see Figure 2). Note that the crosspieces at Stations 1 and 2 are placed at the forward side of the marks and the Station 3 mold on the after side of the mark. Check that these crosspieces are square to the sides.

4. Set the ladder jig on sawhorses, and level it both crosswise and lengthwise. Screw the jig to the sawhorses (see Figure 3). Mark a centerline on each crosspiece.

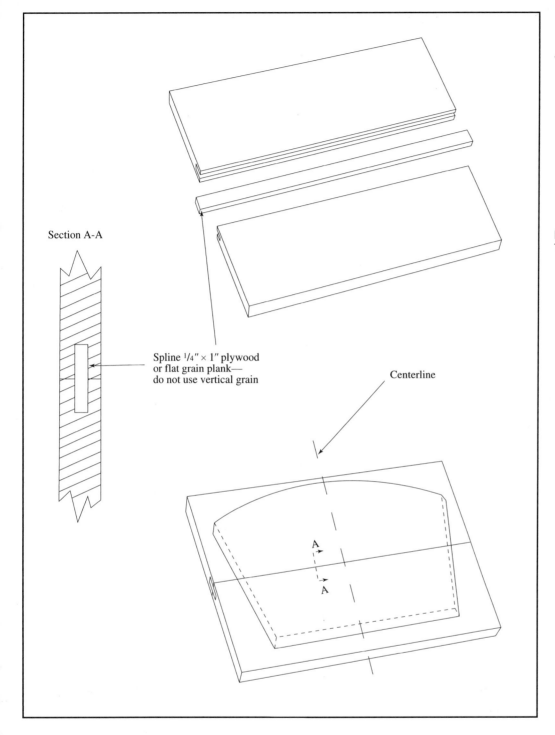

Section A-A

Spline ¹/₄″ × 1″ plywood
or flat grain plank—
do not use vertical grain

Centerline

A
A

Figure 4:
Transom assembly

Step B: Glue up the transom (see Figure 4). If you do not have a large shop or many tools, the first three of the following steps can be jobbed out to a boat or cabinet shop.

1. Joint up one edge of each of the two 4-foot planks (plane the edge square and straight).

2. Cut ¼-inch by ½-inch slots for the spline. Use a router with a slot-cutting bit. A table saw with a dado blade will also do the job.

The planks can also be joined by wood biscuits, using a biscuit joiner, or dowels, using a dowel jig. Nevertheless, I believe a spline works better in this application.

3. Make the spline, ¼ inch by 1 inch by 5 feet (¼-inch plywood or mahogany). This should be a slip fit into the slot. The spline needn't be planed if a gap-filling glue, such as epoxy or plastic resin glue, is to be used.

4. Dry fit the planks and the spline together.

5. Test your clamping system. Put a straightedge across the face of the transom. If it shows there is a bow in the transom, clamp a straight 2 by 4 across the convex side of the bow and pull it down with C-clamps. Protect the 2 by 4 from the glue with plastic or wax paper; also, to prevent the clamps from marring the wood, put scrap wood pads under the C-clamps.

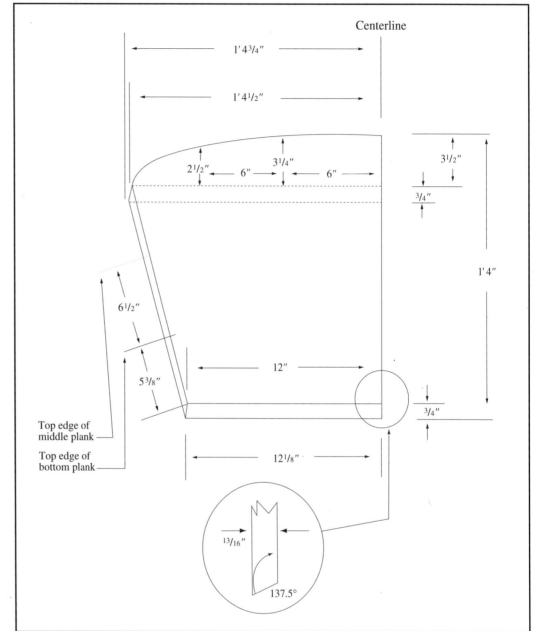

Figure 5:
Transom dimensions

6. When all is ready, take your transom setup apart, apply glue, and reclamp. Follow the instructions on the glue container carefully. Most glues require a temperature of 70 degrees; this can be critical for some types of glues (epoxies in particular). I have found that plastic resin glue (Weldwood is one of the common brand names) is more forgiving than epoxy and have used it successfully in an unheated shop.

When using glues, safety is a critical concern. Vapors from epoxies can cause allergic reactions. Also, there have been reports that epoxies can be carcinogens. To be safe, you need proper ventilation, a mask that provides protection from chemical fumes, and chemical-resistant gloves.

Prompt cleanup is important, as hardened glue can be difficult to remove. Use solvents recommended by the manufacturer. Plastic resin glue cleans up well with warm water. Even while cleaning up use proper protective gear and ventilate the work space well.

7. Store the glued-up transom in a warm place overnight.

Step C: Shape the transom.

1. With your (sharp!) block plane held at a 45-degree angle to the run of the grain, smooth any unevenness at the glued spline joint. Go over the entire transom with a finish sander; begin with 80-grit sandpaper, then finish with 100-grit.

2. Mark a centerline (see Figure 5).

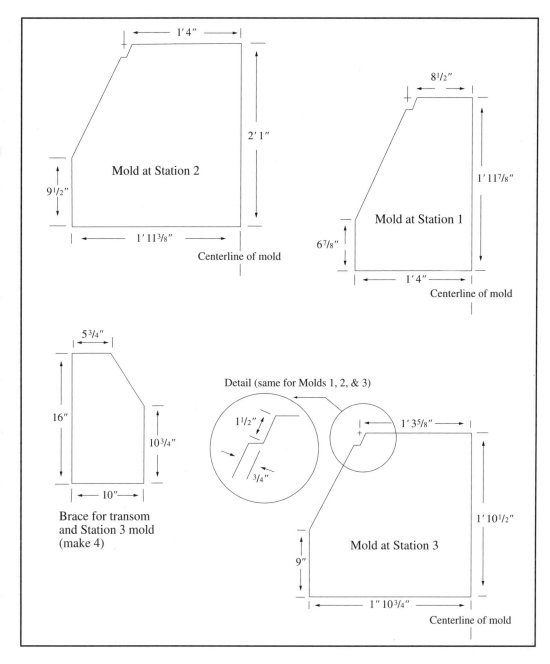

Figure 6:
Mold dimensions

3. Draw the outside dimensions of the transom using the centerline as a reference.

4. Draw the inside dimensions.

5. Cut to the outside lines, but leave the lines.

6. With your block plane and spokeshave, plane from the outside lines to the inside lines. Leave the top of the transom square for now. You can dress it down after the boat has been planked and is turned over.

Step D: Mark centerlines on the molds, and cut out the molds and mold braces (see Figure 6).

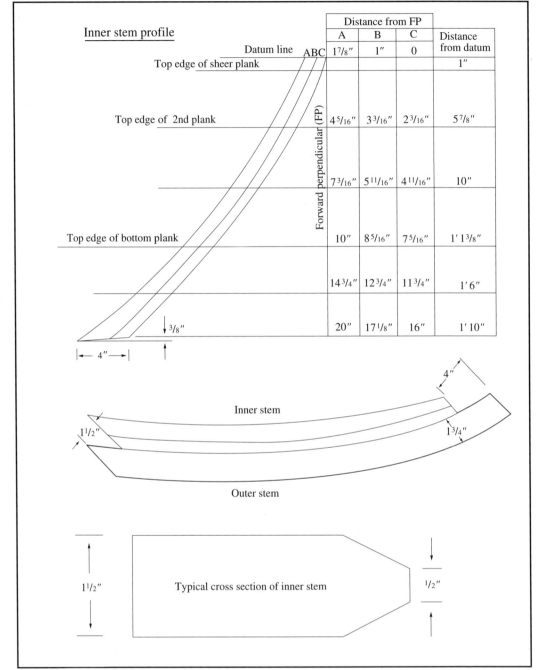

Figure 7: Stem dimensions

Inner stem profile

	Distance from FP			Distance from datum
	A	B	C	
Datum line ABC	$1^7/8''$	$1''$	0	
Top edge of sheer plank				$1''$
Top edge of 2nd plank	$4^5/16''$	$3^3/16''$	$2^3/16''$	$5^7/8''$
	$7^3/16''$	$5^{11}/16''$	$4^{11}/16''$	$10''$
Top edge of bottom plank	$10''$	$8^5/16''$	$7^5/16''$	$1'\,1^3/8''$
	$14^3/4''$	$12^3/4''$	$11^3/4''$	$1'\,6''$
	$20''$	$17^1/8''$	$16''$	$1'\,10''$

Forward perpendicular (FP)

$3/8''$

$\leftarrow 4'' \rightarrow$

Inner stem

$4''$

$1^1/2''$

$1^3/4''$

Outer stem

Typical cross section of inner stem

$1^1/2''$

$1/2''$

Step E: Make a pattern of the shape of the inner stem with poster board (see Figure 7). Do not cut line B; this is a guideline for the stem bevel. Mark the shape of the inner stem on the stem stock. Leave enough room on the stock to draw a curved line 1¾ inches away from line C, and parallel to it, after line C is cut on the bandsaw. Extend this line 1½ inches past the heel of the inner stem and 4 inches past its top. This is the shape of the outer stem. The angles at the top and bottom of the outer stem are the same as the angles at the top and bottom of the inner stem.

Step F: Cut out the inner stem at lines A and C, and mark line B on both faces. Mark where the upper edge of the planks intersect the stem as shown on Figure 7. On the face of the stem at C, mark lines ½ inch from each edge; mark a centerline down the face as well. Bevel the stem from line B to the ½-inch line on the face of the stem (see the typical cross section detail in Figure 7).

Step G: Cut out the outer stem to the lines made in step E and set it aside.

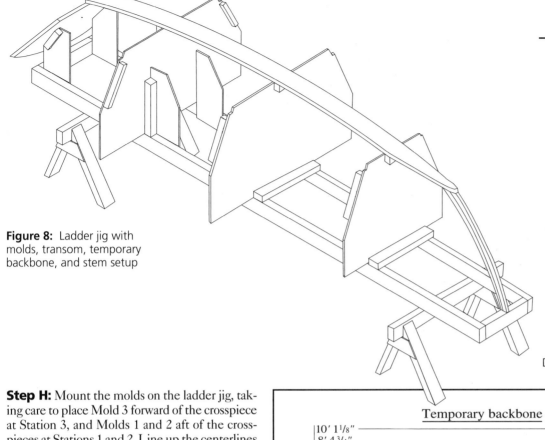

Figure 8: Ladder jig with molds, transom, temporary backbone, and stem setup

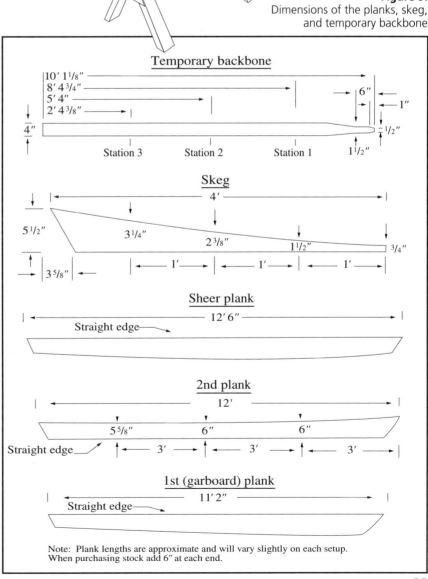

Figure 9:
Dimensions of the planks, skeg, and temporary backbone

Step H: Mount the molds on the ladder jig, taking care to place Mold 3 forward of the crosspiece at Station 3, and Molds 1 and 2 aft of the crosspieces at Stations 1 and 2. Line up the centerlines on the molds with the centerlines on the crosspieces. Fasten with 1 ½-inch drywall screws. (See Figures 2 and 8.)

Step I: Mount and fasten the braces at the transom and Mold 3 with 1½-inch drywall screws. Make sure that the braces are square to the ladder jig (see Figure 2).

Step J: Cut out 1½-inch-square clamping blocks from lumberyard 2 by 4s. Fasten the clamping blocks on the edges of the molds and the transom braces. Use this same stock to screw the braces at Mold 3 to Mold 3. Fasten with 1½-inch drywall screws (see Figures 3 and 8). Screw through the molds into the brace screw blocks.

Step K: Cut out the temporary backbone (see Figure 9) and mark on it the transom and mold locations as indicated. Taper this backbone to 1½ inches at the forward end to fit over the stem. Do this carefully as it is critical to a good setup. The backbone will hold the molds at the proper spacing until the bottom is planked.

Step L: Set up the backbone and the molds (see Figure 8).

1. Screw the temporary backbone to the transom and the stem with 1½-inch drywall screws. Be sure that the transom is square to the backbone and that the centerline of the backbone is directly over the centerline of the stem.

Note: Plank lengths are approximate and will vary slightly on each setup. When purchasing stock add 6" at each end.

2. When this assembly is mounted on the molds, the stem should hit the forward end piece of the ladder jig and the transom should fit snugly on the transom braces. The centerline on the transom should line up with the centerline on the ladder jig, and the transom braces should be equidistant from the centerline on the transom. A level placed on the centerline of the transom should show it to be plumb.

3. When all fits properly, line up the centerline on the stem with the centerline on the forward cross-piece, drill, and fasten. (These are temporary fastenings, so use drywall screws.)

4. Temporarily screw the transom to the transom braces after you have aligned as described in Step 2. If you intend to varnish the transom, however, clamp it to the transom braces so the final finish will not be marred by filled screw holes.

Step M: With your level, check that the molds are vertical. Bevel and fit the screw blocks between the molds and the backbone. Fasten the blocks to the molds with 1½-inch drywall screws (see Figure 8). Adjust the molds to line up with the station marks on the backbone. Remember that the station line on the backbone at Station 3 fits on the after face of Mold 3. The marks on the backbone at Stations 1 and 2 fit at the forward faces of Molds 1 and 2. Screw the backbone to the screw blocks on the molds.

Step N: Check the setup and make adjustments to it until the answer to each of the following questions is "Yes."

1. Do the centerlines on the molds and the transom check out vertically when tested with the level?

2. Are the tops of the molds and the transom level as checked with the spirit level and by sighting across them?

3. Are the molds square to the jig?

4. Place the level vertically alongside the stem. Does it show the stem to be plumb?

5. Spring a batten through the chine notches and against the top corners of the transom and the stem. Mark where it intersects the transom and the stem. Try it on the other side. Is the length between marks the same? Repeat this test at the sheer.

6. When everything checks out, the setup is complete.

IV

Fitting the Garboards and the Chines

Boat jargon

Chine — The line formed by the meeting of the side and the bottom. The chine is also the fore-and-aft framing member to which the side and bottom planks are fastened.

Garboard — Plank 1, the first side plank, the one whose lower edge is fastened to the chine.

Note: Plank 1, or the garboard, is actually two planks, one on each side of the boat, mirror images of each other. The same is true for Planks 2 and 3.

Materials required

Garboard planks — two pieces cedar, spruce, or Eastern white pine, ½ inch by 8 inches by 14 feet.

Chines — one piece mahogany or oak, ¾ inch by 6 inches by 12 feet.

Step A: Fair the stem and transom edges (see Figure 10).

1. Lay a batten across the molds, the transom, and the stem. It should lie tightly across the bevels at the stem and the transom in the area from the bottom of the boat to the top edge of the garboard plank.

2. If the batten does not lie properly, work the stem down, using a spokeshave and a block plane, until it does. Check your work by moving the batten up and down along the stem and molds, keeping the batten parallel to the ground.

3. Repeat the operation at the transom. To check the results, bend your plank stock around the boat and clamp it in place. It should fit tightly at the stem and transom.

- Boat jargon
- Materials required
- Fair the stem and transom edges
- Fit the garboard
- Mark the chine pocket
- Cut the chine pocket
- Make the chines
- Take off the bevels needed to fit the chines
- Cut the forward bevels
- Fit the chines
- Fair the chines
- Hang the garboard

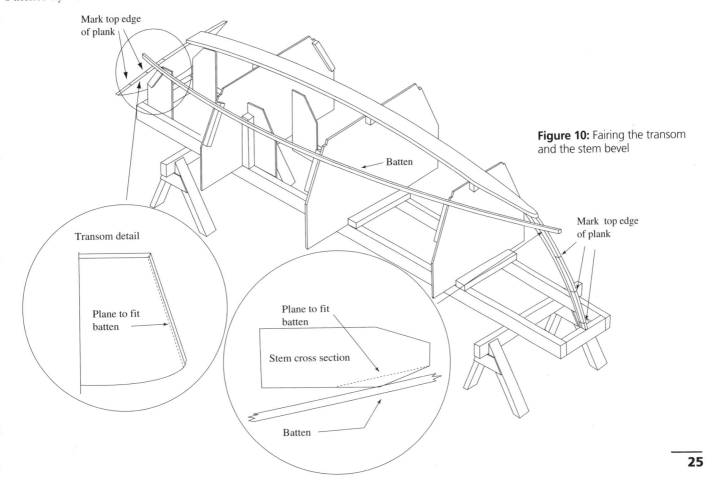

Mark top edge of plank

Batten

Transom detail

Plane to fit batten

Plane to fit batten

Stem cross section

Batten

Mark top edge of plank

Figure 10: Fairing the transom and the stem bevel

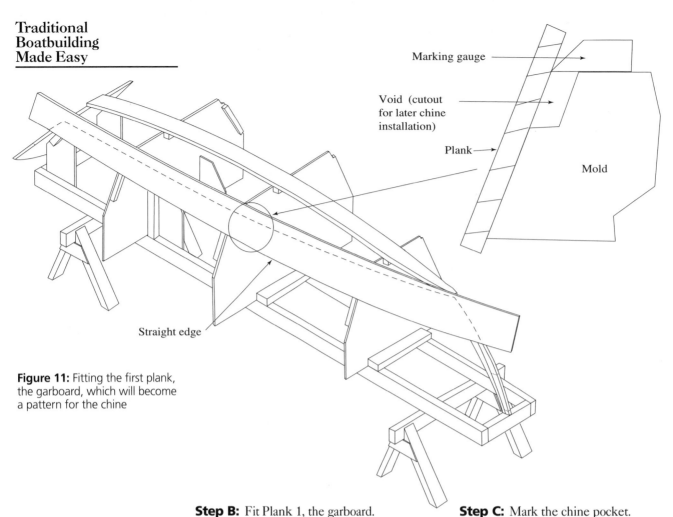

Marking gauge

Void (cutout
for later chine
installation)

Plank

Mold

Figure 11: Fitting the first plank,
the garboard, which will become
a pattern for the chine

Straight edge

Step B: Fit Plank 1, the garboard.

1. Make sure the plank stock has one straight edge (see Figure 9).

2. Place the plank stock on the molds, straight edge down, and line up the bottom edge, fore and aft, with the appropriate marks on the stem and the transom. Clamp it in position, making sure that it covers the upper corners of the molds (see Figure 11).

3. Mark the transom and stem boundaries on the ends of the plank's upper edge. Mark for the top of the stem and the transom. At each mold, mark the intersection of the top of the mold with the inner face of the plank (note the use of a marking gauge for this purpose shown in Figure 11).

4. Remove the plank and drive a nail at each mold mark on the plank and on the marks locating the tops of the transom and stem. Spring a batten alongside the nails and mark the line.

5. Cut to the line at the stem and along the bottom edge of the plank. Leave about ¼ inch extra at the transom for fine tuning.

6. Try this plank on both sides of the setup. It should fit with very little difference between the sides. Make a mate to this plank for the other side of the boat. If you are unsure of the fit, leave a slight margin around the cut edge. Try out this plank and mark any changes you might have to make.

Step C: Mark the chine pocket.

1. The after end of the chine, which is cut square, fits into a pocket cut into the top corner of the transom. Study Figures 12 and 13. Mark a line with your combination square on the top edge of the transom ¼ inch from the after edge and 90 degrees to the side (see Figure 13). Extend in this line at least ¾ inch from the corner.

2. Mark a line ¾ inch parallel to the top corner of the transom and another on the forward face of the transom parallel to the side and ¾ inch away from it (see Figure 13). Extend this last line down the forward face of the transom 1½ inches.

3. Measure down 1½ inches from the top of the transom along its outboard edge and mark a point on the forward corner of the transom.

4. Using your bevel gauge, pick up the bevel between the top and side of Mold 2. Mark this bevel on the forward face of the transom, starting from the point located in Step 3 and crossing the line marked in Step 2 (see Figure 13).

5. Check your results against the illustration. If it looks good, we're ready to proceed.

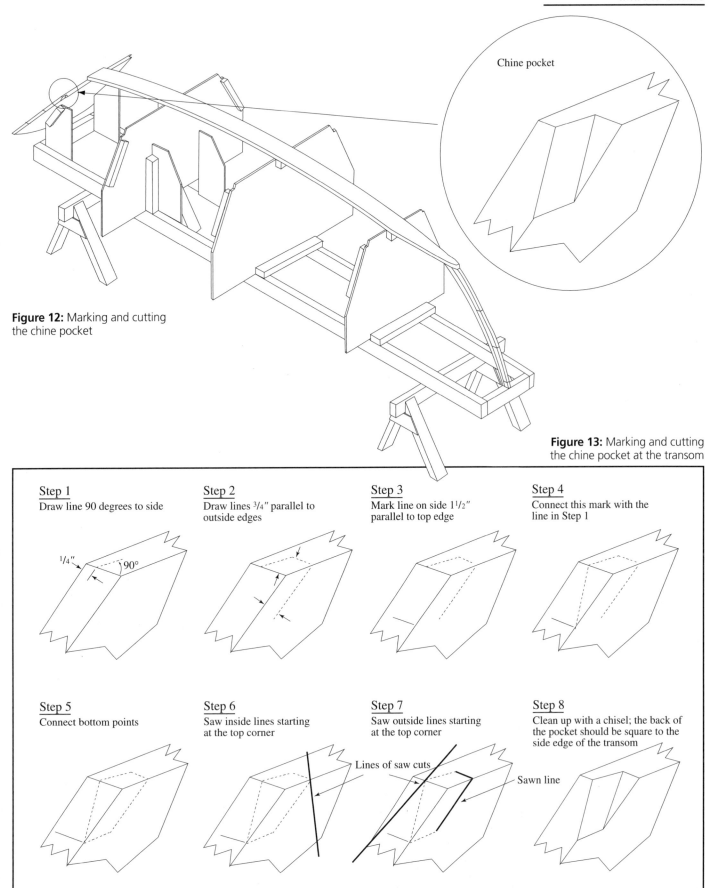

Chine pocket

Figure 12: Marking and cutting the chine pocket

Figure 13: Marking and cutting the chine pocket at the transom

<u>Step 1</u>
Draw line 90 degrees to side

<u>Step 2</u>
Draw lines ³/₄″ parallel to outside edges

<u>Step 3</u>
Mark line on side 1¹/₂″ parallel to top edge

<u>Step 4</u>
Connect this mark with the line in Step 1

¹/₄″   90°

<u>Step 5</u>
Connect bottom points

<u>Step 6</u>
Saw inside lines starting at the top corner

<u>Step 7</u>
Saw outside lines starting at the top corner

Lines of saw cuts

<u>Step 8</u>
Clean up with a chisel; the back of the pocket should be square to the side edge of the transom

Sawn line

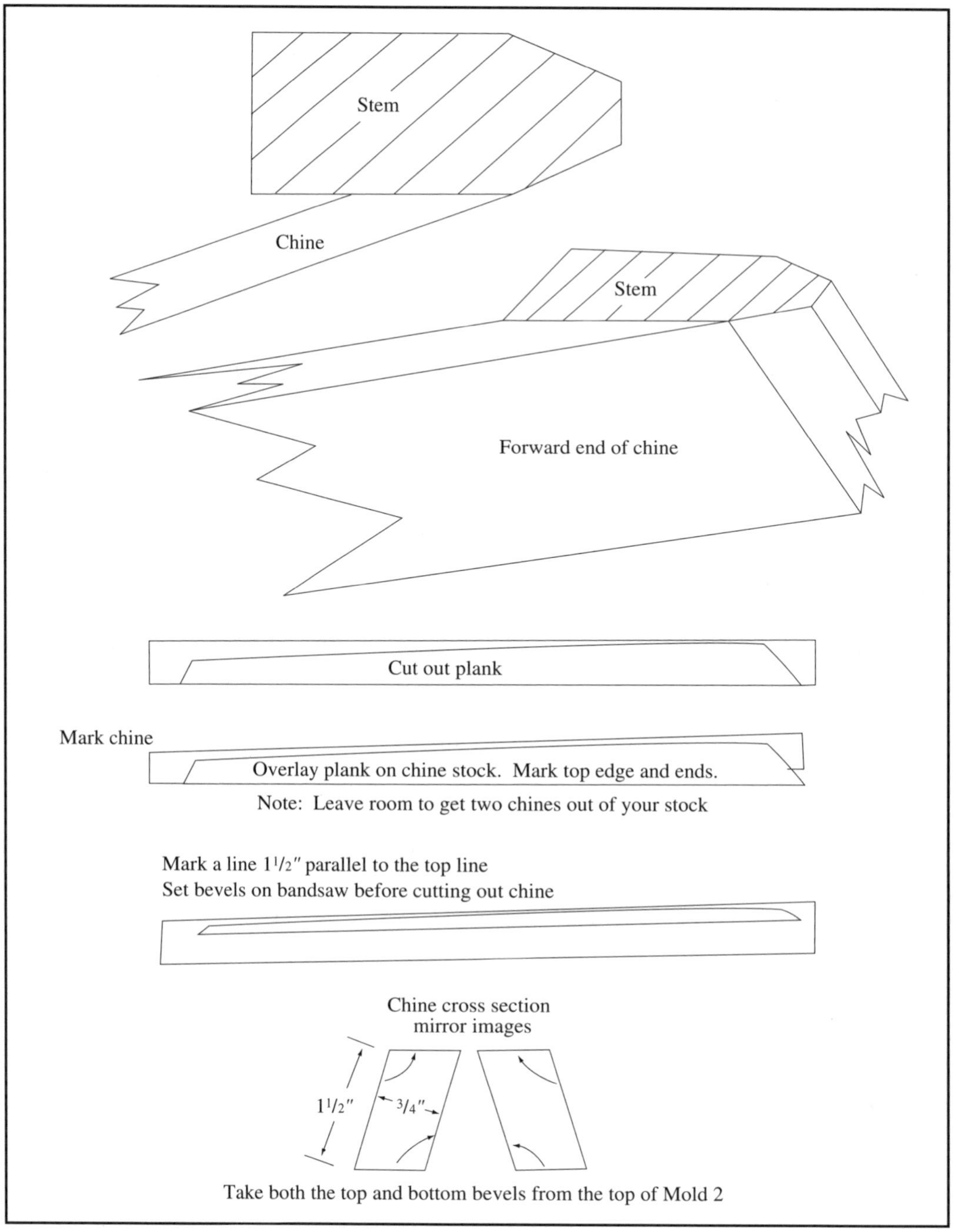

Figure 14:
Shaping the chine and fitting the
forward end to the stem

Stem

Chine

Stem

Forward end of chine

Cut out plank

Mark chine

Overlay plank on chine stock. Mark top edge and ends.

Note: Leave room to get two chines out of your stock

Mark a line 1½″ parallel to the top line
Set bevels on bandsaw before cutting out chine

Chine cross section
mirror images

1½″   ¾″

Take both the top and bottom bevels from the top of Mold 2

Step D: Cut the chine pocket.

1. We'll be using a dovetail saw, a fine-tooth back saw, or Japanese pull saw. If you aren't experienced with these tools, you might want to practice. Study Figure 13 carefully before you cut, and leave the lines when you cut.

Cut the lines on the top and forward face of the transom, starting at the top corner of the pocket. Then cut the lines at the top and side, also starting at the top corner. Clean up the pocket with a sharp chisel. The back of the pocket should be at a 90-degree angle to the side edge of the transom.

2. Repeat this operation on the other side.

Step E: Make the chines.

1. The bottom edge of the plank (the chine edge) becomes the pattern for the shape of the chine.

2. Place the plank on the chine stock. Be sure to locate it near the top of the stock so you can get two chines out of the same piece (see Figure 14).

3. Mark the edge that corresponds to the bottom of the boat first, then mark the ends for the stem and transom.

4. Move the plank down 1½ inches and draw another line to represent the other edge of the chine.

5. With your bevel gauge, measure the angle between the side and the bottom of the boat at Mold 2 (the center mold). Set this bevel on your bandsaw (or panel saw or sabersaw) and cut out the chine carefully, leaving the pencil lines. Remember that the bevels are parallel! Cut the stem line and the transom line square. If there is any difference between the left and right sides of the boat, take care to use the proper length for each side.

6. Keep in mind that the goal is to make two chines that are mirror images of each other and that it is easy to make a mistake here. You will have to feed the second chine through the saw from its opposite end so the bevels will be correct. Study Figure 14 carefully. Before you cut the second chine, put the first chine on the setup to confirm the direction of the bevels. If you still have doubts, make a test on a piece of scrap wood. Good luck!

7. When the chines are cut out, place them on the molds to see how they fit. Mark which edge is up and which is down. The down edges can be planed smooth and sanded, and the inboard corners, which will be exposed in the boat, can be rounded slightly. The upward-facing edges will be planed to a changing bevel after the chine is fitted.

Step F: Take off the bevels needed to fit the chine (see Figure 14).

1. Spring the batten from the transom around the molds to the stem. Push it up until it is just below the chine notches in the molds and the transom, and temporarily clamp it in place. When the forward end of the batten reaches a point 1½ inches down the stem, the batten simulates the bottom outside corner of the chine. It is important that the batten accurately reaches the stem at the same location as will the chine, so fit it carefully. If necessary, hold the chine on the setup to check the point of intersection at the stem.

2. With your bevel gauge, pick up the bevel formed by the side of the stem and the batten (see Figure 14). Be sure to hold the bevel gauge in the same plane as the bottom of the boat.

3. Mark this bevel on one chine at its forward end. Mark both the top and the bottom, and connect the ends of these lines with a line on the back of the chine. Do the same on the other chine.

4. Remove the batten.

Step G: Cut the forward bevels.

1. Before you cut the forward chine bevels, put the chines on the setup to check that the bevels have been marked the correct way.

2. Clamp the chine firmly to your bench. Using a fine-tooth back saw, dovetail saw, or Japanese pull saw, cut the bevel. Start at a corner and leave the line. Repeat on the opposite chine. Clean up the bevel to the lines with your block plane.

Step H: Fit the chines.

1. Place one of the chines on the setup, in the chine notches in the molds. The forward end of the chine should now fair into the beveled edge of the stem, and the garboard should be able to fit tightly over the face of the chine and stem without leaving a gap. If a correction to the bevel is necessary, use your low-angle block plane. Plane the top of the chine near the stem so its bevel is in the same plane as the top of the stem. After both chines are in place, a straightedge should fit across both chines and the stem with no gaps. Make sure that the chine will bend in a fair curve through the chine notches after the forward end is fastened.

2. Once the bevel fits at the stem and at the top, drill a pilot hole, and screw the chine snugly against the stem, bedding the chine with compound. Wear chemical-resistant gloves, and clean up any excess immediately.

3. Bend the chine through the notches and past the transom.

4. While holding the chine in place against the transom, mark the back of the chine in the pocket, using the corner of the pocket as a guide.

5. With a combination square held against this line, mark square lines on the top and the bottom of the chine at the transom. Then connect the ends of these lines across the outside face of the chine.

6. Once you are sure your measurements are correct, saw off the end of the chine, starting from a corner as you did at the forward end.

7. Lay one chine in place. If all works well, drill an appropriate hole to prevent splitting, and fasten the chine to the transom with a 1½-inch bronze screw. Bed the chine in the pocket as you did at the forward end, and clean up carefully.

8. Now fit and attach the other chine in the same manner.

9. Make two chine hold-downs from ⅜-inch plywood or ¾-inch wood scrap (see Figure 15) and attach them at each side of Mold 2.

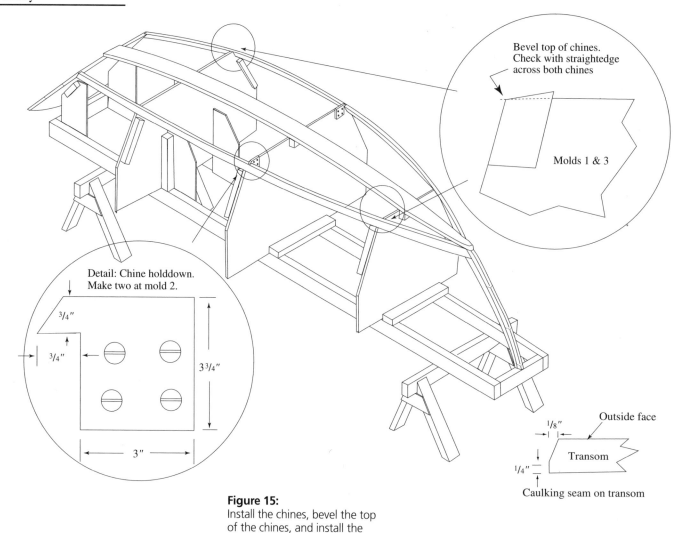

Bevel top of chines.
Check with straightedge
across both chines

Molds 1 & 3

Detail: Chine holddown.
Make two at mold 2.

3/4"

3/4"

3 3/4"

3"

1/8"

Outside face

Transom

1/4"

Caulking seam on transom

Figure 15:
Install the chines, bevel the top
of the chines, and install the
chine hold-down at Mold 2

Step I: Fair the chines.

1. Now you must plane the changing bevel on the top edges of the chines (see Figure 15) so the bottom planks will fit tightly. To do this, lay a straightedge from one side of the setup to the other, across both chines. Plane off the high inside corner of the chines until the straightedge lies flat. Take long fore-and-aft strokes with your plane to maintain a fair surface on the top of the chine. Check regularly as you go with the straightedge.

2. Cut a caulking seam at the transom by drawing a line on the after face of the transom, parallel to the side and top edges, ⅛ inch away. Then draw a line on the side and top edges of the transom ½ inch in from the after face. Plane this off with your block plane (see the detail in Figure 15). The seam so created will be filled with flexible compound only; no caulking cotton is required. You will also cut a similar caulking seam at the stem after the boat is planked.

Step J: Hang the first plank (the garboard).

1. We will now cut the gains on the first plank (see Figure 16). The gains are 1-inch-wide rabbets, 18 inches long, that diminish from the full ½-inch plank thickness to a feather edge at the stem and the transom (i.e., at the extreme ends of the plank). The purpose of the gain is to let the neighboring plank diminish from a full lap to fit flush at the bow and stern.

Cut the gain with your rabbet plane, using an edge guide if you have one. A block of wood clamped to the plank 1 inch in from the edge will work well as a substitute. Study the illustrations carefully before you cut the wood. As a check, mark the location of the gain on the plank with a pencil and hold the plank up to the setup. The planks should be cut off to overhang no more than 1/16 inch at the bow and the stern.

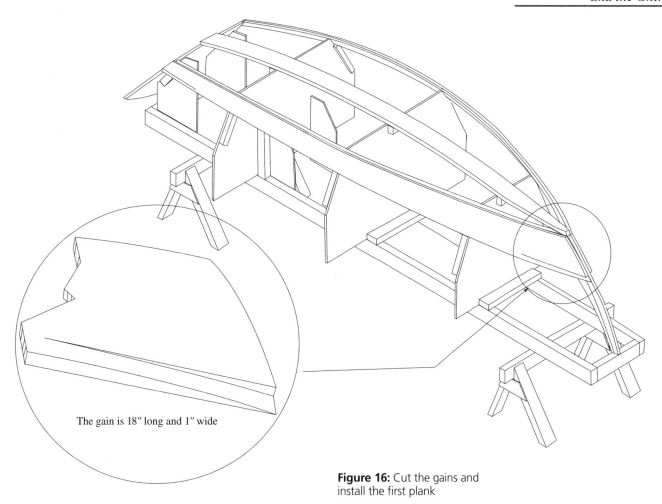

The gain is 18″ long and 1″ wide

Figure 16: Cut the gains and install the first plank

2. With your bevel gauge, take off the bevel between the lay of the plank and the face of the stem (see Figure 16). Plane this bevel at the forward end of the planks or cut them on the bandsaw, but before you do, check the planks on the setup to ensure that you bevel the correct side of each plank. The purpose here is to cause the forward ends of the planks and the face of the stem to form a flat surface for the subsequent fitting of the outer stem.

3. Mark the screw locations for the stem and the transom on the ends of both planks; they should be 1 inch apart and ½ inch in from the edge. Allow a little extra at the transom if your plank overhangs somewhat. The locations for the screws along the chine should be ¾ inch from the bottom edge of each plank, 3 inches apart.

4. Now hang the planks. Clamp them in place, starting from the bow and working to the stern, making sure they touch the molds naturally, without forcing. If a plank does not touch the molds, you will have to release the clamps and reset the plank until it does. Make sure that the ends are on the marks you made on the stem and transom.

5. When the planks fit, drill for the fastenings, then take the planks off and apply bedding compound on the stem, transom, and chine. Level the compound with a putty knife to about ¹⁄₁₆ inch thick. Then, one side at a time, hang the planks, screwing them down with 1-inch #8 bronze screws along the bottom and 1¼-inch #8 screws at the stem and the transom. Immediately clean up the first plank completely with solvent before hanging the plank on the other side. Wear gloves and ventilate the work area well.

V

The Bottom Planks

There are two possible methods for planking the bottom. We will consider both. The first method is the traditional cross-plank bottom, which is suitable for those who will be leaving their boat in the water or who will otherwise be able to keep the planking from drying out; the second is a plywood bottom, which is best for those who will be trailering or cartopping their boats.

Boat jargon

Scarf — A joint for joining two pieces of wood end to end; in this project such a joint is made by beveling and gluing.

Green — Newly set-up glue or resin that has not yet cured to full strength.

Materials required

Cross-plank bottom — planking stock, ¾ inches by 4 to 5 inches, approximately 75 linear feet; one pound 1½-inch #10 bronze ring nails.

Plywood bottom — one sheet 5-ply high quality marine ply, ⅜ inch by 4 feet by 8 feet; one pound 1¼-inch #12 bronze ringnails.

Step A: Cross planking the bottom.

1. Plane a ⅛-inch caulking seam on the top of the side planks, the full width of the plank (see Figure 17).

- **Boat jargon**
- **Materials required**
- **Cross planking the bottom**
- **Laying the alternate plywood bottom**

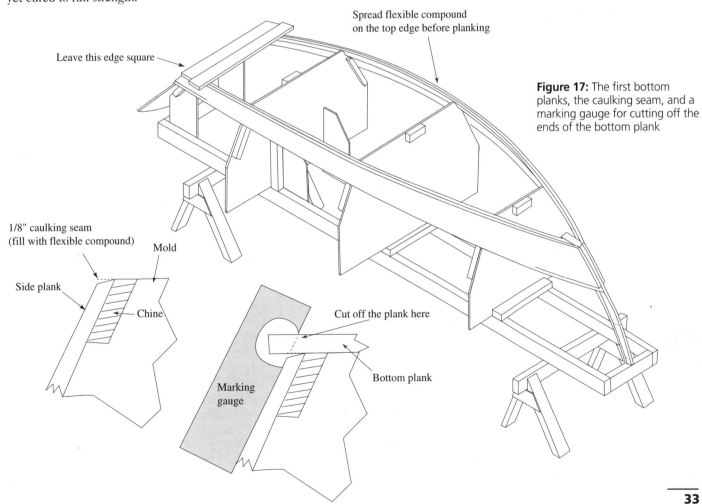

Spread flexible compound on the top edge before planking

Leave this edge square

Figure 17: The first bottom planks, the caulking seam, and a marking gauge for cutting off the ends of the bottom plank

1/8" caulking seam (fill with flexible compound)

Side plank

Mold

Chine

Marking gauge

Cut off the plank here

Bottom plank

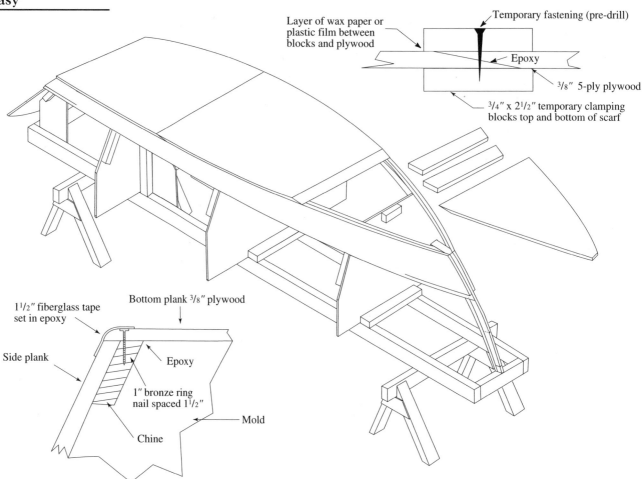

Layer of wax paper or
plastic film between
blocks and plywood

Temporary fastening (pre-drill)

Epoxy

³/₈″ 5-ply plywood

³/₄″ x 2¹/₂″ temporary clamping
blocks top and bottom of scarf

1¹/₂″ fiberglass tape
set in epoxy

Bottom plank ³/₈″ plywood

Side plank

Epoxy

1″ bronze ring
nail spaced 1¹/₂″

Chine

Mold

Figure 18: Fitting and finishing off the alternate plywood bottom

2. Cross planking is accomplished by laying on the bottom ¾-inch planks with widths of 4 inches to 5 inches. These planks are fastened at each end to the chines with three or four 1½-inch #10 bronze ring nails. Drill for the nails before driving them.

To select a drill for proper thickness, hold it alongside a nail and sight against a light. You should see the rings of the nail clearly on each side of the drill, while the body of the nail will be obscured by the drill. If in doubt, drill into a piece of scrap wood, drive a nail, and evaluate the result.

3. Remove the temporary backbone and chine hold-down clamps. Start planking from the stern and work forward, pulling each new plank tightly against the last installed plank with clamps and wedges. Do the best you can, but don't worry about slightly open seams. The bottom planking will swell considerably when immersed, and small gaps will close.

Leave the after end of the first plank square at the transom so you will have a good land for your nails. (The ends of the planks at the sides, after they are fastened, will be beveled to match the angle of the side planks as they meet the bottom.) Bed the ends in way of the side planks and the chines with compound, and be sure to fill the caulking seam. Clean up immediately.

4. To cut off the ends of the planks, use a gauge to mark the top of the cut (see Figure 17) and use your 10-point handsaw. Turn the saw so its teeth are up, lay the flat side of the saw against the side plank, and, holding the saw lightly there with one hand, saw up from the underside. Thus the side plank will act as a guide to achieve the proper bevel for the ends of the bottom planks; they will be smoothed up with a block plane later.

5. Continue planking this way. Force the planks tightly together with clamps and/or wedges before nailing. Be careful not to get lumps of compound between the planks.

6. As you get near the bow, calculate the number and widths of the planks required to fill the remaining space so you won't be left with a forward plank that is too narrow.

7. After the bottom is planked, clean up the ends of the bottom planks with your low-angle block plane so they are flush to the side planks. The work will be easier if you hold the plane at a 45-degree angle, facing down. Leave the edge of the bottom at the transom square, but round off the corner a little. Fair the forward plank into the stem face so the outer stem will fit tightly over it.

Step B: Laying the alternate plywood bottom (see Figure 18).

1. Five-ply plywood has three of its plys running lengthwise, which makes this the stiffest dimension. Since there will be no framing in the bottom of this boat, we will use this stiff dimension to our advantage by planking across the boat. Starting from the stern, lay the sheet of plywood with its outer grain running across the boat and mark the edges on its underside. Make marks on the chines at the forward edge of the plywood.

2. Take the plywood to a pair of sawhorses and cut outside the lines with your sabersaw or fine-tooth circular saw.

3. Drill pilot holes for 1¼-inch #12 bronze ring nails, one at each corner. Choose your drill as in Step A-2 above, so the nails will fit tightly in the pilot holes. At the forward end, make sure that the pilot holes are 2 inches away from the edge. Drill pilot holes every 1½ inches at the stern and the side.

4. Bevel the after edge of the plywood to match the bevel of the transom.

5. We will be scarfing the pieces of plywood together (see Figure 18), so mark a line 2 inches from the forward edge on the top surface of the plywood. On the bench, clamp a piece of wood to the bottom of the forward edge to prevent the feather edge from breaking off and plane the bevel.

6. Mix enough epoxy glue to cover the edge of the transom and the chines up to the marks you made at the forward end of the plywood. Thicken the glue with wood flour (fine, sifted sawdust), silica, or microballoons, and spread it on the chine, side plank edges, and transom. Lay the glue on so there will be squeeze-out when the bottom is fastened down. Wear gloves, a vapor-proof mask and ventilate well.

7. Put this first plywood bottom plank on the boat and, when you are satisfied it lies properly, fasten it down at the corners. Then drive nails along the edges at the transom and the chines every 1½ inches. Clean up squeezed-out glue immediately.

8. Lay the remainder of the sheet of plywood on the bottom with the grain going across the boat and overlapping the scarfed edge of the first piece. Carefully align its straight edge along the scarf bevel. Mark the edges as above.

9. Take the plywood off the boat and cut to the lines, leaving the marks. Mark and cut a 2-inch scarf on the bottom side of the plywood along the after edge. Then mark and cut another 2-inch scarf on the top face of the forward end of the piece.

10. Place this piece back on the boat and check the scarf to make sure you have a tight fit. Drill pilot holes in the four corners and along the sides. The pilot holes in the after corners should go through the scarf, and the forward pilot holes should be 2 inches back from the forward edge of the plywood so they will be clear of the scarf.

11. Now is the time to glue up and fasten the second plank as you did the first.

12. The scarf, which is also glued at this time, must be clamped together while the glue sets up. This is done by drilling pilot holes and driving drywall screws through two pieces of wood, 2 to 2½ inches wide and ¾ inch thick, that run along the length of the scarf, one over and the other under the joint (see Figure 18). The screws, if they are long, can be driven clear through all three pieces. There is no need to fasten these scarfs with permanent screws or nails if you use a waterproof epoxy glue. This rig will be removed after the glue sets up, so be sure to place wax paper or plastic between the wood pieces and the plywood so they don't become a permanent part of the boat.

13. Now fit the last bottom piece in the same manner as the first two. Check to see that your scarf fits tightly, drill pilot holes, then glue and fasten it in place. Clamp this scarf as you did the first one.

14. The next day after gluing up, take out the temporary screws and remove the clamping pieces. Whittle out some softwood plugs, dip them in thickened epoxy, and tap them lightly into the holes left by the screws. After the glue dries, cut off the ends of the plugs with a sharp chisel and sand smooth. Clean up the cured glue on the scarf with your block plane (set for a light cut and held at 45 degrees) followed by a belt sander using a 100-grit belt; sand with the grain. Then go over the scarf with a finish sander and 150-grit sandpaper.

Now plane the edges of the plywood bottom flush to the sides, and round them off to a radius of about ½ inch at the sides and the transom. Leave the forward edge of the bottom flush to the stem, so the outer stem will fit tightly.

15. With 1½-inch fiberglass tape set in epoxy, overlap the rounded-off edges at the transom and sides. As soon as the epoxy is hard enough — though still green, as it is easier to work then — fair out the hard edges of the tape with a sharpened paint scraper that has been ground to a slightly convex curve. Be careful not to gouge the side plank. After the epoxy has fully cured, fair the surface with a finishing sander and 100-grit sandpaper.

VI

The Remaining Side Planks, the Keel, and the Skeg

Materials required

Side planks — four pieces cedar, spruce, or Eastern white pine, ½ inch by 8 inches by 14 feet

Skeg and keel — hardwood stock, ¾ inch thick

Fastenings — clench nails, or ½-inch copper tacks; 3-inch bronze wood screws; assorted bronze wood screws

Step A: Add shims for Plank 2 (see Figure 19).

1. Cut enough ⅝-inch-wide strips from ½-inch plank scrap to shim out the molds from the edge of the garboard plank (Plank 1) to the sheer.

2. Drill and fasten the shims with drywall screws.

Step B: Fit Plank 2, one on each side of the boat.

1. Check to see that each of the remaining plank stock has one straight edge. If not, plane one edge of each piece straight and square.

2. Set your combination square at 1 inch, and using this as a guide, mark a line on the bottom edge of the garboard plank from the forward gain to the after gain.

3. Place a piece of plank stock on one side of the boat, making sure that it lies flat on the molds and that the ends overlap the stem and the transom. The straight edge should be facing toward the bottom of the boat. Clamp the plank stock in place; the straight edge should lie close to the line you drew in Step 2. If the ends do not fit tightly into the gains on the garboard plank, adjust the fit with your block plane.

4. Check the fit at the transom. Use your block plane to adjust the transom edge bevel if necessary. Adjust the caulking seam at the same time if necessary.

- **Materials required**
- **Add shims for Plank 2**
- **Fit Plank 2**
- **Shim for Plank 3**
- **Fit Plank 3**
- **Plane fair the ends of the planks**
- **Fit the keel and the skeg**
- **Fit the outer stem**
- **Shape the outer stem**
- **Fasten the outer stem**

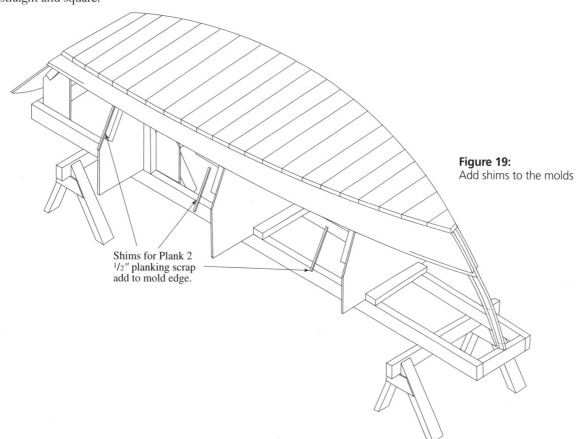

Figure 19:
Add shims to the molds

Shims for Plank 2
½″ planking scrap
add to mold edge.

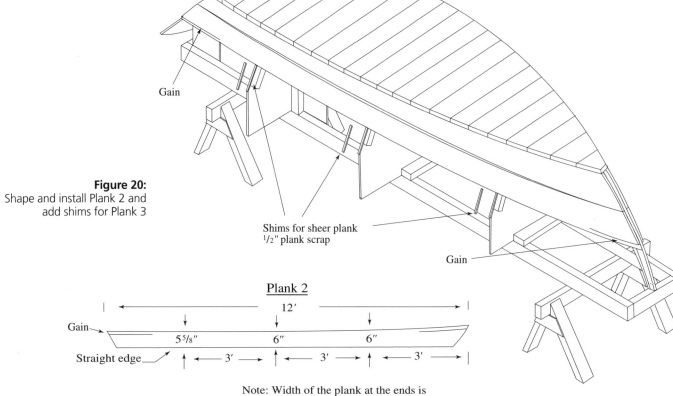

Figure 20:
Shape and install Plank 2 and
add shims for Plank 3

Gain

Shims for sheer plank
1/2" plank scrap

Gain

Plank 2

12'

Gain

Straight edge

5 5/8"   6"   6"

3'   3'   3'

Note: Width of the plank at the ends is
taken off the marks on the stem and transom.
The other dimensions are at the mold locations.

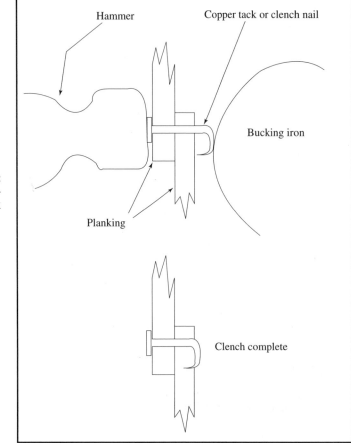

Hammer   Copper tack or clench nail

Bucking iron

Figure 21:
Clenching a cop-
per nail or tack

Planking

Clench complete

5. Mark the outer edges of the stem and the transom on the ends of Plank 2, and transfer the
marks showing the top limits of the plank that you
marked on the transom and stem. Then mark
lines across the plank at the locations of Molds 1,
2, and 3, using the mold edges as guides.

6. Remove the plank and mark the plank widths
along the mold lines from the straight edge (see
Figure 20).

7. Spring your batten down the plank so it hits the
width marks and the marks at the stem and transom. Sight the line and correct it for fairness, then
mark the line.

8. Cut out the plank, leaving the lines. Plane the
long edge fair, but do not plane the ends at this
time.

9. Check the plank on both sides of the boat to
insure that it will fit. If it does, use it as a pattern
to make a plank for the other side.

10. To make sure you cut the gains in the right
place, put the planks on the boat and mark gain
locations (see Figure 20). Then cut the gains as
you did for the garboard planks.

11. Clamp the planks on the boat, making sure
they fit tightly into the gains on the garboard
planks. When you are satisfied they fit properly,
drill and fasten the planks at the stem and the
transom with 1 1/4-inch #8 bronze screws.

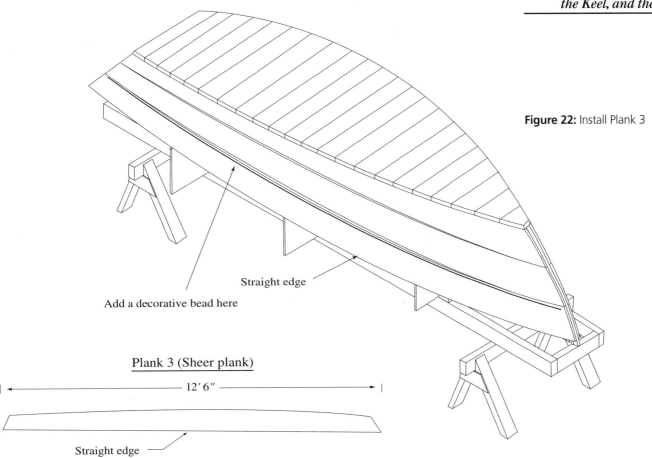

Figure 22: Install Plank 3

Straight edge

Add a decorative bead here

Plank 3 (Sheer plank)

|←————— 12′ 6″ —————→|

Straight edge

12. One at a time, unfasten the plank ends, leaving the plank clamped at the molds, and squeeze bedding compound along the stem and the transom, and in the gains. With a putty knife, level the compound to a depth of $\frac{1}{16}$ inch.

13. Refasten each end after it is bedded, and clean up as you go. Leave in place the clamps holding the planks to the molds.

14. Now is the time to clench nail the overlapping edges of the garboard (Plank 1) and Plank 2. Figure 21 shows the technique.

Copper is quite soft, so clench nailing is easy, though you would be wise to practice first with some plank scrap. Drill a pilot hole for each fastening. As you tap the fastening through the pilot hole, hold a bucking iron (see Figure 21) so the fastening hits it and bends away from the edge of the plank. As the fastening continues to bend its point will be forced back into the plank, becoming, in effect, a one-sided staple. With a little practice, you can make the fastenings appear uniform on the inside of the boat.

15. Before you clench the plank laps, you must mark the locations of the frames. As you will screw through the laps into the frames, it is not necessary to clench nail where the frames will lie.

Begin measuring for the frames at a position 2 inches aft of Mold 3. Mark a line parallel to the mold, then continue forward at 18-inch intervals, marking lines parallel to the molds, across the planks. There are seven frames on each side.

The frames closest to the bow may have to be slanted, or canted, slightly forward to position the heels of the frames so you can put fastenings in them. They are canted for visual reasons as well: in the flare of the bow, if the frames are installed parallel to the amidships frames, they will look as if they are tilting aft, and we don't want that. Frames that are canted are called, logically enough, cant frames.

Measure the positioning of the frames on both sides carefully, and cross check by measuring from both the stem and the stern. This is critical, as we want the frames on both sides to be the same distance apart, with the exception of the forward frames, which should be canted forward until they are eye sweet and their heels can be properly fastened.

16. Once the frame locations are marked, divide the spaces between the frames evenly at about 3-inch intervals for the clench nails. Mark $\frac{1}{2}$ inch in from the lapped plank edge for the pilot holes, drill, and clench.

Step C: Shim for Plank 3.

1. Prepare and install the shims for Plank 3, just as you did for Plank 2 (see Figure 22).

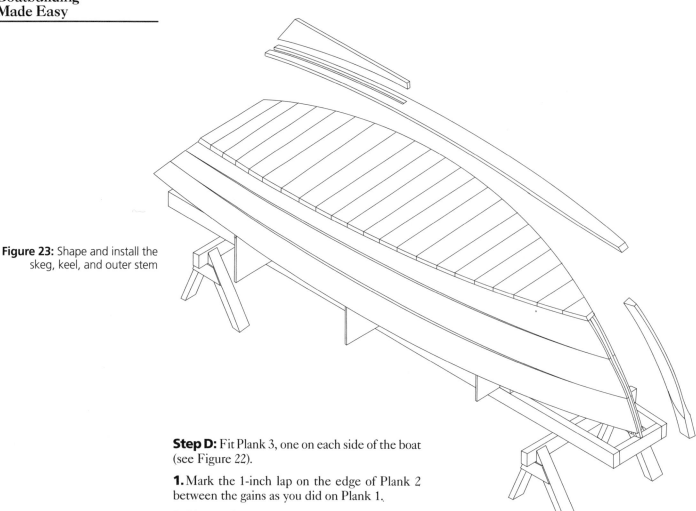

Figure 23: Shape and install the skeg, keel, and outer stem

Step D: Fit Plank 3, one on each side of the boat (see Figure 22).

1. Mark the 1-inch lap on the edge of Plank 2 between the gains as you did on Plank 1.

2. Place a piece of plank stock on one side of the boat, this time with the straight edge facing down toward the sheer. Line up the straight edge with the sheer marks at the bow and the stern. Be sure that the top edge of this plank overlaps the plank lap marked on Plank 2 in Step 1.

3. Since this plank will overlap the gain, it will lie at an angle at the transom and stem. To correct for this, wedge up the plank at the bow and the stern so it lies parallel to the edge of the transom and stem.

4. Reach under the boat and, using the edge of Plank 2 as a guide, mark a line on Plank 3. Then mark for the bow and the stern ends as before.

5. Remove the plank. Add 1 inch to the line you marked under the boat to allow for the width of the lap. Then cut to this line and the marked lines at the ends. Check this plank on both sides of the boat to insure that it will fit. If it does, use it as a pattern to make a plank for the other side.

6. Plane fair the long cut edge.

7. A nice detail for this boat is to plane or rout a $3/8$-inch bead along the bottom outside edge of Plank 3 — the edge of the plank opposite the sheer edge (see Figure 22). Later, this bead can be painted a color that contrasts with the rest of the planking.

8. Install these planks as you did Plank 2. Before you clench, remember to mark the frame locations and not to clench there.

Step E: Holding your block plane at a 45-degree angle and pushing from the outside into the boat, plane fair the ends of all the planks at the transom and stem.

Step F: Fit the keel and the skeg (see Figures 23 and 24).

1. The keel is $3/4$ inch by $3½$ inches. Check the length by placing the stock on the boat and marking the ends.

2. Bevel the forward end of the keel to fair into the inner stem, so the outer stem will fit tightly over the end of it.

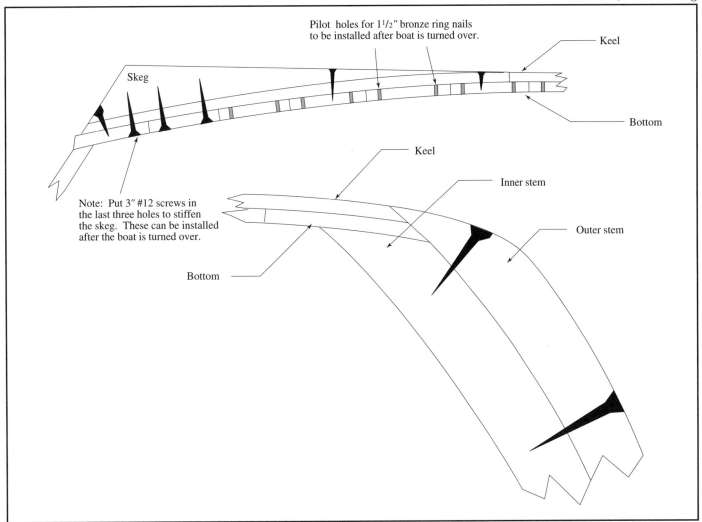

Pilot holes for 1½″ bronze ring nails
to be installed after boat is turned over.

Keel

Skeg

Bottom

Note: Put 3″ #12 screws in
the last three holes to stiffen
the skeg. These can be installed
after the boat is turned over.

Keel

Inner stem

Outer stem

Bottom

3. Taper the last 3 feet of the keel at the bow down to 1½ inches so it will fair into the outer stem (see Figures 23 and 24).

4. Starting at the transom, cut a ¾- by 4-inch slot in the keel, as shown in Figure 23.

5. Using the measurements provided (see Figure 9), mark the shape of the skeg on ¾-inch stock. Check to see that it is long enough to fit into the slot in the keel. Cut out the skeg and fair it with your plane. Check the curve of the bottom of the skeg against the bottom of the boat; adjust the fit if required.

6. Mark a centerline on the bottom of the boat, and then measure out from this line 1¾ inches on each side. This is the footprint of the keel. Now drive pilot holes through the bottom, ¾ inch in from the lines defining the outside edges of the keel. These holes are for nails that will be driven through the bottom into the keel after the boat has been turned over. For a plywood bottom, the pilot holes should be driven at 6-inch intervals; for a planked bottom, drive two holes per plank.

7. Fair and sand the transom end of the keel, and round over the outside edges of the keel by ⅛ inch.

8. Place the keel on the bottom and line up its centerline with that of the bottom of the boat. Drill and fasten the keel to the bottom with a 1¼-inch #8 bronze screw at the bow and at the forward end of the slot. If the boat is cross-planked, drive a screw roughly every 2 feet into the center of a bottom plank. If the boat has a plywood bottom, screw through from the inside of the boat into the keel with 1-inch #8 bronze screws.

Note that these screws are used to hold the keel in place until the boat has been turned over and the keel has been further fastened with nails driven through the bottom from inside the boat.

9. Position the skeg, drill, and fasten it (see Figure 24).

10. Pull in the sides of the keel in way of the slot and fasten from the outside enough to hold it until the boat is turned over.

Figure 24: Fasten the skeg, and fasten and round off the stem. Note the pilot holes in the bottom for the ring nails, which will be installed after the boat is turned over.

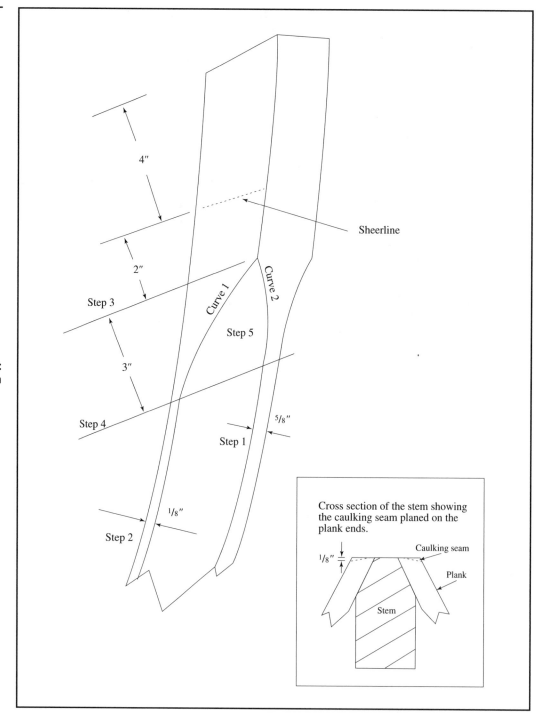

Figure 25:
The shape of the outer stem

Sheerline

Curve 1

Curve 2

Step 3

Step 5

Step 4

Step 1

Step 2

4″

2″

3″

5/8″

1/8″

Cross section of the stem showing
the caulking seam planed on the
plank ends.

1/8″

Caulking seam

Plank

Stem

Step G: Fit the outer stem (see Figures 23, 24, and 25).

1. Get out the blank for the outer stem you cut earlier. With your block plane and spokeshave, fair up the inside and outside faces.

2. Check the fit of the outer stem on the boat. The fit needn't be perfect, just close (less than 1/16 inch). The stemhead should extend about 4 inches past the sheer for later finishing. Check to see that the total width of the faces of the inner stem and the plank ends are the same as the width of the outer stem. If wider, mark the width of the outer stem on the offending planks and plane down the thickness of those planks at their forward ends with your block plane. Once the stem is in place you will not notice that this adjustment has been made. Sand the planed area smooth with 100-grit sandpaper.

3. Mark an 1/8-inch caulking seam along the bow ends of the planks. Plane this seam the full width of the plank edges (see Figure 25). This seam will be filled with flexible compound; no caulking cotton is necessary.

Step H: Shape the outer stem.

1. Mark two lines ⅝ inch apart down the middle of the face of the outer stem (see Figure 25).

2. Extend the sheerline across the stem.

3. Draw a line parallel to the sheerline, 2 inches below it.

4. Draw a line parallel to the above line, 3 inches below it and across the face of the stem.

5. Draw the following curves and make poster board patterns of them (see Figure 25):

A curved line that is eye-sweet (Curve 1 on Figure 25).

Another curved line from the upper point of Curve 1 to the intersection of the 3-inch line and the ⅝-inch line at the same side of the stem (Curve 2 on Figure 25).

Using your patterns mark these curves on one side of the stem. Eyeball them carefully to make sure they are fair and look good. If not, modify the patterns and re-mark the stem. When you like the results, use the patterns to mark the other side of the stem.

6. Carve the stem to shape with your spokeshave and plane. Use a file where the curve is too great for the spokeshave. Sand and round off the outside corners by ⅛ inch.

Step I: Fasten the outer stem.

1. Place the outer stem on the boat, drill, and temporarily fasten it to the inner stem with five 3-inch bronze screws. When you are satisfied with the fit, remove the stem, apply flexible compound, and refasten.

2. Clean up excess bedding compound immediately.

3. Holding the side of your handsaw flat on the keel as a guide, saw off the overhanging heel of the outer stem. Round over fore and aft until it fairs with the adjoining pieces (see Figure 24). Sand smooth.

VII

Turning Over the Boat, Fitting the Quarter Knees and Breasthook

In this chapter the finished boat begins to emerge. As you shape the knees, stemhead, and frames, you will have the opportunity to add your own personal touches to the design. Take time to contemplate possible embellishments and have fun with them.

Materials required

Temporary cross brace — at least ¾ inch by 3½ inches by 4½ feet.

Quarter knees and breasthook — hardwood stock, ¾ inch thick.

Stemhead — hardwood stock, 1½ inches thick.

Step A: Before turning over the boat we need to make and install a temporary cross brace to keep the boat's shape until the internal framing and seats are installed (see Figure 26). This brace should be located 3 inches aft of Mold 2. It can be made from any stiff piece of wood that is as long as the boat is wide. It needn't be over 4 inches wide or ¾ inch thick.

1. Mark the edge of the sheer on both sides of the boat 3 inches aft of Mold 2. Hold the piece of wood you have selected as a cross brace across the boat at this point and mark where it intersects the inside corners of the sheer plank.

- **Materials required**
- **Make and install a temporary crossbrace**
- **Remove the molds**
- **Measure, make, and install the breasthook**
- **Complete the stemhead**
- **Measure and install the quarter knees**

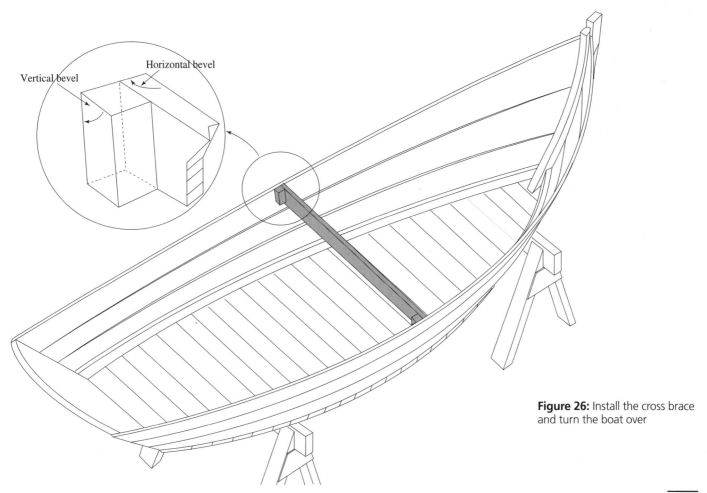

Figure 26: Install the cross brace and turn the boat over

2. With your bevel gauge take off the bevels between this cross brace and the sheer plank (see Figure 26 for a detail of these bevels). Take off the vertical bevel parallel to the mold, and the horizontal bevel at 90 degrees to the mold, facing aft at the sheerline. You can record these bevels by marking them on a piece of scrap wood that has a straight edge.

3. Place the cross brace on the bench and mark the vertical bevels at the sheer intersection marks.

4. From scrap, cut two clamping blocks to fasten to the ends of the cross brace.

5. Set the horizontal bevel on the bandsaw and cut the line on the cross brace. Cut the same bevel on the clamping blocks.

6. Screw the cross brace to the clamping blocks with drywall screws.

7. Clamp the cross brace in the boat, taking care to put scrap-wood pads under the clamps to protect the sheer plank. If possible, set the clamps so the adjusting screws are inside the boat so they will not get in your way.

Step B: Remove the molds.

1. Unscrew Molds 1, 2, and 3 at the jig.

2. Unscrew the transom and the stem from the jig.

3. Lift the boat off the jig, turn it upright, and place it on the floor.

4. Disassemble the jig and store the parts out of the way.

5. Now you can drive nails in the drilled holes through the bottom into the keel and skeg. Nail the bottom in sections, using backing blocks under the keel to insure that the nails drive home solidly. For a boat with a cross-plank bottom, use 1¼-inch #10 bronze ring nails (see Figure 24); for a plywood bottom use 1-inch #12 bronze ring nails.

6. Place the boat on sawhorses, using wedges and blocks to stabilize the boat without any twist.

Step C: Measure for the breasthook (see Figure 27), and make and install it.

1. Make the breasthook pattern.

1a. Using poster board, cut out a pattern for the breasthook, which extends 11 inches along each side and fits around the inner stem.

1b. Fit the pattern around the inner stem first, then mark along the inside edges of the sheer planks.

1c. On the pattern draw the shape of the breasthook. Allow at least 11 inches on each side and 5 inches from the stem, aft. Do not cut out this shape yet.

1d. To determine the vertical bevel where the breasthook fits against the inside of the sheer planks, place a piece of scrap plank across the sheer in the area of the breasthook. Then with your bevel gauge, take off the bevel for the edges of the breasthook and record it on a piece of scrap. Be sure that your bevel gauge is held 90 degrees to the face of the sheer plank.

1e. Using the same technique as above, measure the bevel for the forward end of the breasthook where it meets the back of the stem and record it on a piece of scrap.

2. Note in Figure 27 that the breasthook is actually made up of three parts — two halves and a spline joining them. This is done so the direction of the grain in the legs of the breasthook will run parallel to the sheer planks.

To divide the breasthook pattern in half, first measure 11 inches along each side of the pattern, beginning at the forward end. Draw a line across the pattern from point to point. Find the center of this line. Draw a line from this point forward to the stem end of the pattern, dividing it in half.

3. With your bevel gauge measure Angle A, Figure 27. Cut this angle across the breasthook stock. You now have two roughed-out breasthook halves.

4. With your slot cutter cut the slots in the inside edges of the roughed-out breasthook halves. Fit the spline, glue, and clamp; sand when the glue is dry.

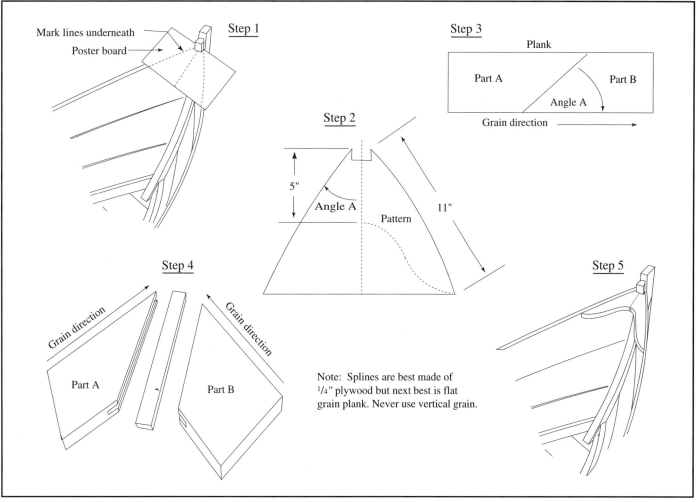

Step 1

Mark lines underneath

Poster board

Step 2

5"

Angle A

Pattern

11"

Step 3

Plank

Part A

Part B

Angle A

Grain direction

Step 4

Grain direction

Part A

Grain direction

Part B

Note: Splines are best made of
¼" plywood but next best is flat
grain plank. Never use vertical grain.

Step 5

Figure 27: Make a pattern and
glue up the breasthook

5. Shape, fit, and fasten the breasthook.

5a. Finish cutting out the pattern.

5b. Using your pattern, mark the proper shape on
the roughed-out breasthook and cut the proper
bevels with a bandsaw.

5c. Fair the curve of the after end of the breasthook with a half-round file and sand smooth.
Round off hard edges ⅛ inch. Fit the breasthook
carefully and make any required adjustments
with your block plane.

5d. Drill for the fastenings and screw the breasthook in place with 1¼-inch #8 bronze screws driven through the sheer planks. Check the fit and
adjust if necessary.

5e. Remove the breasthook, bed it in compound,
and refasten it. Clean up excess bedding compound thoroughly.

5f. Trim the top and the inner stem by laying your
handsaw flat on the breasthook and sawing off the
excess height of the stem. Be careful not to cut
the outer stem.

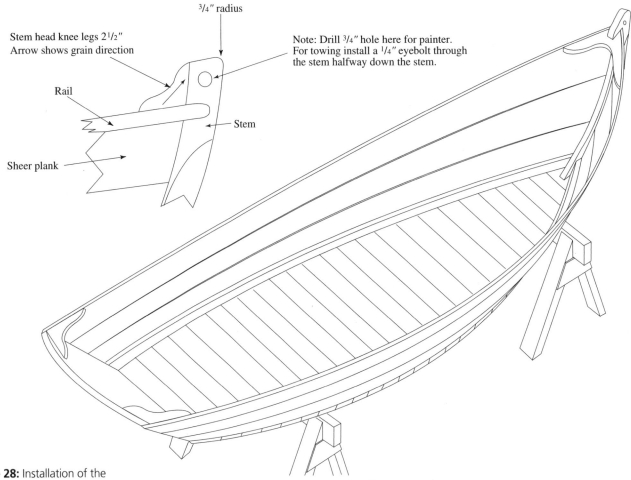

Stem head knee legs 2¹/₂″
Arrow shows grain direction

³/₄″ radius

Note: Drill ³/₄″ hole here for painter.
For towing install a ¹/₄″ eyebolt through
the stem halfway down the stem.

Rail

Stem

Sheer plank

Figure 28: Installation of the
breasthook and quarter knees

Step D: Complete the stem head (see Figure 28).

1. Cut a block of wood beveled to fit the after side of the outer stem, with the grain running in the direction shown in Figure 28. The legs of this knee should be approximately 2½ inches long. Design a nice shape for this piece, as well as the outer stem head.

2. Drill, bed in compound, and install the stem head knee with two 3-inch bronze screws.

3. Finish shaping the stem head knee, then sand, rounding off the hard edges ⅛ inch.

4. Drill a ¾-inch hole in the stem head for the painter (tie-up line). To make sure the hole runs straight and true, locate hole centers on each side of the stem head and drill halfway in from each side, meeting in the middle. Use your combination square as a guide to hold your drill square. Clean up the hole with a round file.

5. Sand off the hard edges of the stem head by ⅛ inch.

Step E: Measure and install quarter knees (see Figures 28 and 29).

1. Cut out a piece of poster board at least 8 inches by 10 inches.

2. Place this pattern stock on top of the sheer plank and against the transom, angled so it is slightly above level (see Figure 29). You decide what looks best. (When we built the original Heidi, the bevel was 77 degrees.) When you have the angle you like, be sure one edge of the poster board is tight to the transom, then mark the edge of the sheer plank on the poster board. Also mark a line on the transom where the pattern hits, so you can locate this line again. Measure the bevels at the transom and the side, and record these bevels on a piece of scrap.

3. Draw the shape of the knee on the pattern. The sheer leg is shown as 9 inches and the transom leg as 6 inches. Feel free to change these dimensions to suit your eye.

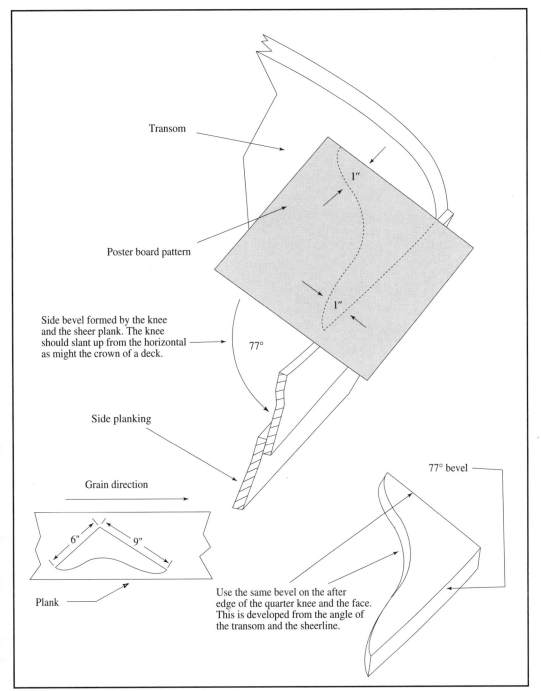

Transom

Poster board pattern

1"

1"

Side bevel formed by the knee
and the sheer plank. The knee
should slant up from the horizontal
as might the crown of a deck.

77°

Side planking

Grain direction

6"   9"

Plank

77° bevel

Use the same bevel on the after
edge of the quarter knee and the face.
This is developed from the angle of
the transom and the sheerline.

Figure 29:
Make a pattern for the quarter
knees and take off bevels

4. Cut out the knee. For looks, I like to bevel the
curved cut at the transom leg so it more or less
matches the rake of the transom, and gradually
decrease the bevel as the curve runs into the sheer
leg of the knee. This is cut parallel to the transom
bevel. Make a mirror image of this knee for the
other side of the boat.

5. Clean up the bandsaw marks on the curved
part of the knee with your block plane and spokeshave. In the tightly curved areas, a half-round
file works best.

6. Check the knees for final fit, then drill, bed in
compound, and fasten. Clean up excess bedding
compound immediately.

IIX

The Frames, Risers, Seats, and Oarlock Pads

Materials required

Frames — oak or mahogany, ³⁄₄ inch thick.

Risers — fir or mahogany, ⁵⁄₈ inch thick.

Center seat — planking stock, ³⁄₄ inch thick by 9 inches wide.

Bow and stern seats — planking stock, ¹⁄₂ inch thick.

Oarlock pads — hardwood, ³⁄₄ inch thick.

Step A: Fit the frames (see Figures 30, 31, and 32).

1. Run a straightedge through the marks you made on the outside of the planks at the laps, indicating the frame locations, and decide whether you still agree with the frame locations or not.

2. If the locations look good, drill through the laps for the fastenings, which will be 1¹⁄₂-inch #8 screws.

3. On the inside of the boat, mark parallel lines ³⁄₄ inch apart, centered on the pilot holes at each frame location.

4. Cut up lengths of ³⁄₄- by 1¹⁄₂-inch plank scrap, approximately 2 feet long.

5. Place these mock frames over the frame locations and eyeball them to see how they lie. Are they evenly spaced on both sides? Make adjustments if necessary, then clamp them in place (see Figure 31).

6. Cut squares of poster board and fit them to each of the straight surfaces of the chine and planks, alongside the mock frames. When the squares fit tightly, staple them to each mock frame, then mark on it the number of the frame and the side of the boat it came from. These are the patterns for the frames.

- **Materials required**
- **Fit the frames**
- **Fit the risers**
- **Fit the after seat cleat**
- **Fit the framing for the forward and after seats**
- **Fit the after seat**
- **Fit the forward seat**
- **Fit the center bench seat**
- **Fit the guardrails**
- **Fit the knees for the center bench seat**
- **Fit the oarlock pads**
- **Fit the stem and skeg bands**

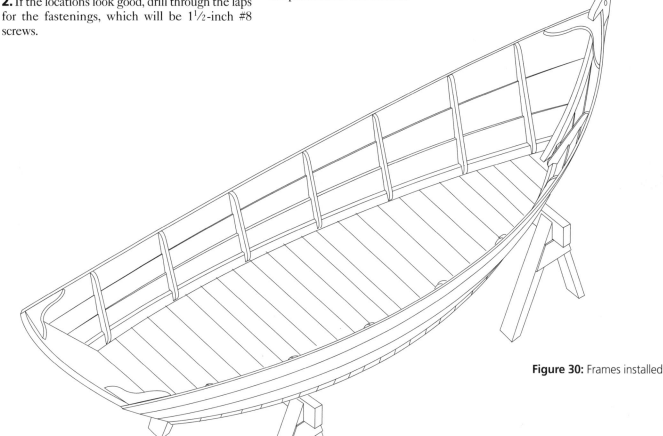

Figure 30: Frames installed

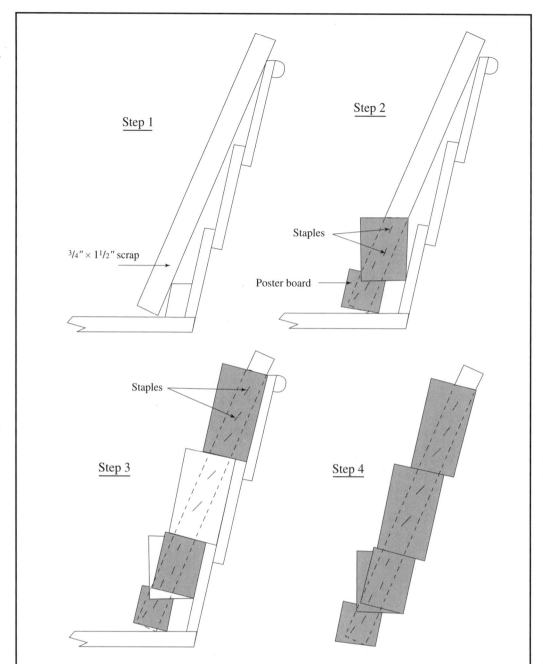

Figure 31:
Making the frame template

Step 1

³/₄″ × 1¹/₂″ scrap

Step 2

Staples

Poster board

Step 3

Staples

Step 4

7. To make a frame, trace around the appropriate pattern on the frame stock. Mark ¾ inch at the chine and at the sheer (see Figure 32). Draw a straight line between these points and finish off with attractive rounds at both ends.

8. Make poster board patterns of the rounds at the ends of your first frame, so you can duplicate them on the rest of the frames.

9. Cut out the frame and fit it. Clean up bandsaw marks and sand the frame smooth, rounding exposed hard corners ⅛ inch. Fasten as shown in Figure 32, from the outside of the planking, through the laps, into the frame. Do not drive a screw at the sheer, however; this will be done when you fasten the rail.

10. Repeat this process for each frame (see Figure 30).

Step B: Fit the risers (see Figure 32 and 33).

1. The risers, which support the seats, extend from 4 inches forward of the forwardmost frame to 4 inches aft of the aftermost frame on each side of the boat. The cross section of the risers is ⅝ inch by 1¾ inches, with the inside corners rounded or chamfered; alternatively, the top can be beveled to fit the seats. If you have a beading plane or beading router bit, a nice detail would be to add a bead on the bottom corner of the riser as shown in Figure 32.

2. Measure and cut the lengths required for the risers, using the appropriate stock, and rip each piece to 1¾ inches wide. Shape them to suit your taste.

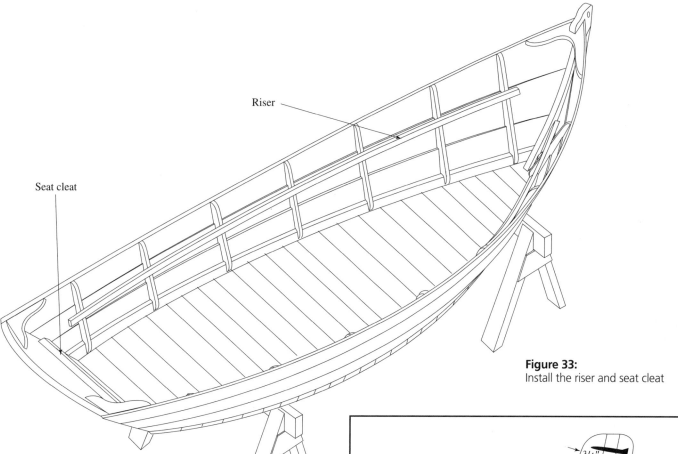

Figure 33:
Install the riser and seat cleat

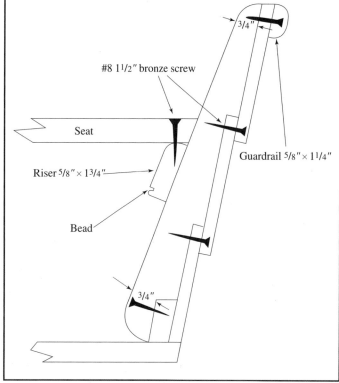

Figure 32: Install and fasten the frames. Seat and riser detail.

3. For most of the length of the boat, the height of the risers is set so the top of the seats will be approximately the same height as the top edge of Plank 2. At the aftermost frame they might extend lower than that line. Do not force the risers edgewise when you bend them. Check to make sure that both risers are the same height.

4. Drill and fasten the risers with 1¼-inch #8 bronze screws.

Step C: Fit the after seat cleat (see Figure 33).

1. The after seat cleat supports the after end of the after seat planks. It is located by placing a straightedge along each riser in a fore-and-aft direction until it touches the transom. Mark this point on both sides of the transom and draw a straight line between the two points.

2. The cross section of the after seat cleat is ¾ inch by 1¾ inches, and the cleat is beveled at the top so the seat planks will fit on top of both the riser and the cleat. This bevel is measured by setting the straightedge along the riser until it touches the transom and recording the bevel thus

formed with your bevel gauge. This bevel can be cut on a table saw or bandsaw. Plane the cut edge smooth, and round off the exposed corners.

3. The cleat, after it is sanded smooth, is fastened to the transom, under the line you marked there.

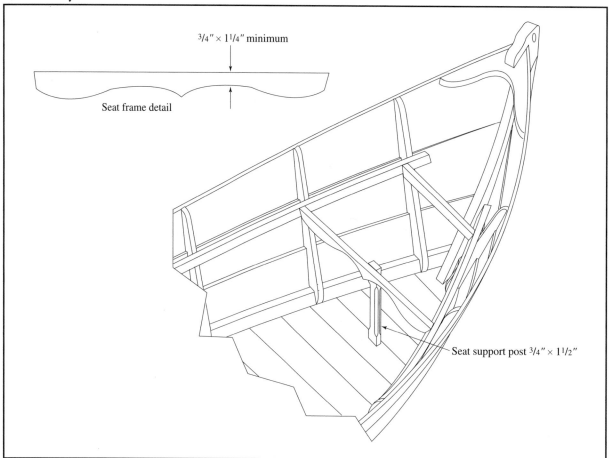

Seat frame detail

$3/4'' \times 1 1/4''$ minimum

Seat support post $3/4'' \times 1 1/2''$

Figure 34:
Install the forward seat frame

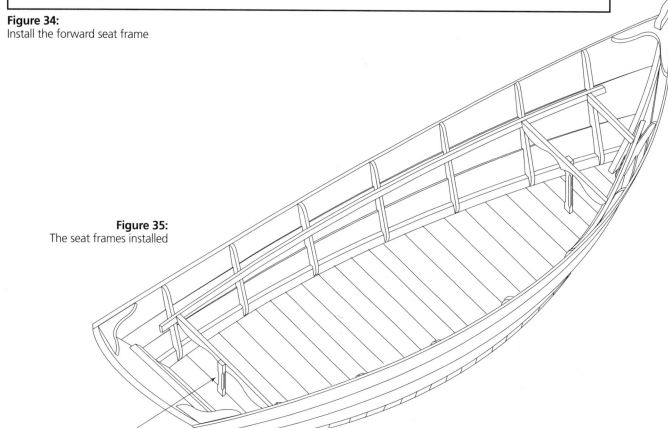

Figure 35:
The seat frames installed

Install stern seat post here.
Detail same as forward post.

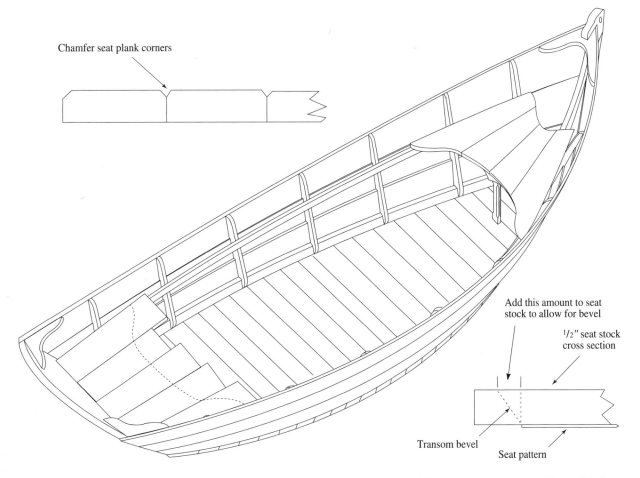

Chamfer seat plank corners

Add this amount to seat
stock to allow for bevel

$^{1}/_{2}''$ seat stock
cross section

Transom bevel

Seat pattern

Figure 36: Stern seat installation

Step D: Fit the framing for the forward and after seats (see Figures 34 and 35).

Please note that if you intend to install a sailing rig, the forward seat should be built heavier than is indicated here, which is for the rowing-only version. Read about the sailing rig in Chapter 11 before you continue.

1. The forward and after seats are built of $^{1}/_{2}$-inch planking stock or any other lightweight stock. The seat cross braces are cut from $^{3}/_{4}$-inch by $2^{1}/_{2}$-inch stock. (For the rowing version see Figure 37; for the sailing version see Figures 46 and 47.)

2. The first step is to build the supporting frame. We will build the frame for the forward seat first. The cross braces are fitted just aft of Frames 1 and 2, placed so a fastening can be driven at an angle through the riser and into the frame. Fasten with $2^{1}/_{2}$-inch #12 bronze screws.

To measure the cross braces, place the ends of a length of $^{3}/_{4}$-inch by $2^{1}/_{2}$-inch frame stock on top of the risers (see Figure 34). At each end, mark a line on the bottom of the stock where the stock intersects with the riser; with your combination square, transfer this line to the top of the stock. With a bevel gauge, take off the bevel between the stock and the face of the riser. Mark this bevel on the stock, beginning from the line at the top. With a hand saw, cut to the line at each end of the stock and fit.

3. The after cross brace of the forward seat is a good place to add decoration. Use your imagination here. I offer a simple design in Figure 34, but you could embellish it. Be sure that you leave at least $1^{1}/_{4}$ inches at the thinnest areas.

4. The seat support post I show is $^{3}/_{4}$ inch by $1^{1}/_{2}$ inches (do not install this post in the sailing model) and is simple in form. Decorate it by rounding off or chamfering the corners. An attractive alternative is to use a turned post. If you don't have a lathe, you could use stock posts sold in woodworker's supply stores, or scavenge attractive legs from a piece of old furniture. Whatever your choice, you will need three posts, one for each seat (see Figure 35).

5. In the stern only one cross brace is required, as the after seat cleat, already installed, supports the after end of the seat; decorate the cross brace to complement the forward one.

Step E: Fit the after seat (see Figure 36).

1. The best way to lay out after seat is to make a poster board pattern of one-half of it. Later, you can turn the pattern over and use it for the other half.

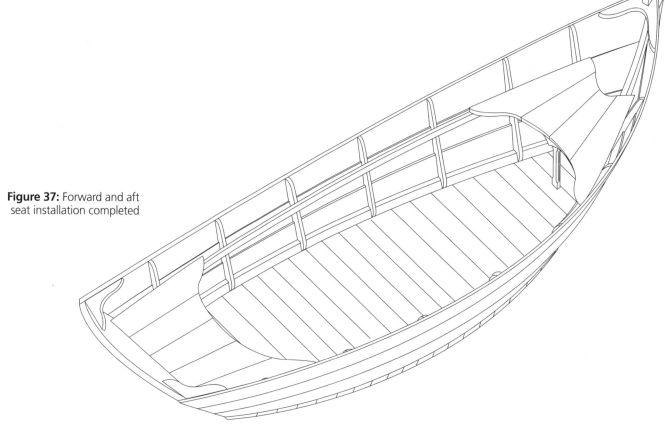

Figure 37: Forward and aft
seat installation completed

2. After fitting the pattern to the transom and the seat riser, draw the curve of the forward edge on the poster board pattern but do not cut it. Decide how far the seats will go past the cross brace along the risers (see Figure 36). Halfway to the next frame might be a place to start. The shallowest part of this curve should overlap the cross brace by at least 1 inch. Experiment with different curves.

3. Do not cut the curve yet. When you decide how far along the risers the seat will go, mark the location on the pattern and draw a line athwartships and parallel to the transom edge of the pattern.

4. Now divide the stern seat into five equal parts, each part wedge shaped, with the small end toward the transom. Check the arrangement for appearance, and adjust until you are happy with it.

5. In the stern, the after end of the seat planks are beveled to fit tightly at the transom (see Figure 37). Since your poster board pattern represents the bottom of the seat and the bevel in the stern adds length to the top of the seat, we need to find out how much extra length must be added to the seat to account for the bevel. First take off the bevel at the transom and mark it on the edge of a piece of seat stock.

6. With your combination square, mark a line from one of the end points of the bevel line square across the piece of seat stock. From this you can calculate how much extra length you must add to the seat planks to allow for the bevel (see Figure 36).

7. You should bevel the outboard edges of the outboard seat planks, where they meet the sides. Use the same method.

8. Using your pattern, mark and cut out the five planks for the stern seat, allowing the planks to extend a little beyond the pattern on both ends. Be sure to add extra length and width for the stern and side bevels. Plane the edges of the planks.

9. Set up the planks on your bench. Place your pattern on the planks and mark the line at the transom. Measure off the extra length allowed for the bevel at the transom and the extra width at the sides. Mark a line parallel to the pattern line.

10. Cut the transom bevel on the ends of the planks and the bevel on the side planks, smooth the cut with your block plane, and fit them into the boat (see Figure 36). Adjust if necessary.

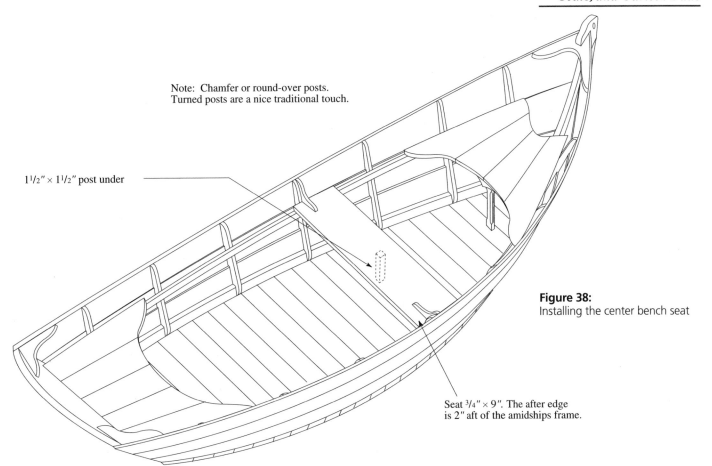

Note: Chamfer or round-over posts.
Turned posts are a nice traditional touch.

$1^1/2'' \times 1^1/2''$ post under

Figure 38:
Installing the center bench seat

Seat $^3/_4'' \times 9''$. The after edge
is 2" aft of the amidships frame.

11. Now draw the forward, curved edge on the seat and cut it out. Smooth that edge with a spokeshave and a half-round file. Bevel or round the corners $^1/_8$ inch.

12. The seats are fastened down with screws that are countersunk just enough so their heads are flush to the seat. This will allow you to remove the seats for refinishing. For appearance, the screws should form an even and pleasing pattern. Lay out the screw pattern on the posterboard pattern first until you like what you see. Then drill and fasten the seat planks with 1-inch #8 bronze screws.

Step F: Fit the forward seat.

1. Make a pattern of the forward seat, which will extend 6 inches forward and aft of Frames 1 and 2 and will overlap the cross braces by 1 inch.

2. Plank the seat with four $^1/_2$-inch planks. Curve the outboard edges to conform to the shape of the risers and bevel those edges to fit against the frames.

Step G: Fit the center bench seat (see Figure 38).

Please note that if you are building the sailing version, go ahead and fit this seat but don't make the post and don't round off the corners until after the daggerboard trunk is fitted.

1. The center seat is made of $^3/_4$-inch by 9-inch stock, with its after edge located 2 inches aft of the center frame. It is installed over a post.

2. To determine the width of the seat, mark the risers 2 inches aft of the center frame and again 9 inches forward of this mark. Measure across the boat from mark to mark at both points.

3. On the stock selected for the seat, measure and mark the forward distance. Find the midpoint of this line and draw a 9-inch line perpendicular to it facing aft. Draw a line parallel to the first and 9 inches away.

4. Measure one-half the distance of the after line from the centerline out. Mark these points.

5. The ends of the seat will be curved slightly to match the sides, and they will be beveled to match the flare of the sides. You will have to add to the length of the seat to allow for the bevel.

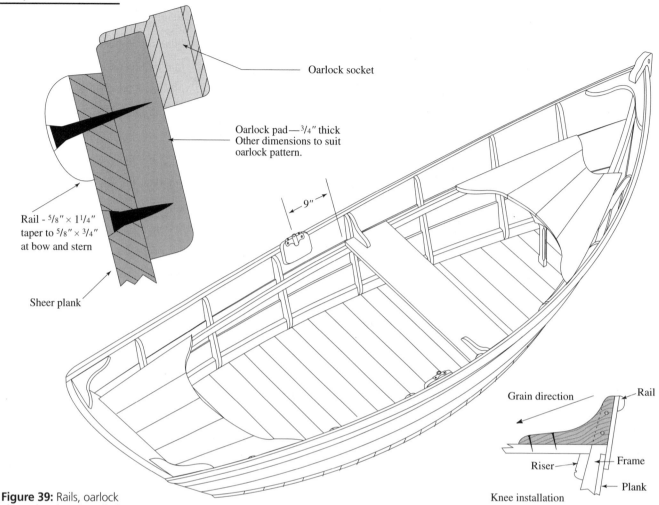

Oarlock socket

Oarlock pad—³/₄″ thick
Other dimensions to suit
oarlock pattern.

Rail - ⁵/₈″ × 1¹/₄″
taper to ⁵/₈″ × ³/₄″
at bow and stern

Sheer plank

9″

Grain direction

Rail

Riser

Frame

Plank

Knee installation

Figure 39: Rails, oarlock
pads, and sockets installed

6. First, determine the curve. This can be done by making poster board patterns. With the patterns draw the side curves between the end points of the seat.

7. Second, put a straightedge across the boat on the risers at the frames. Take off the bevel formed by the seat and the frame and calculate the amount of extra length needed as you did when you fitted the stern seat. Add this distance to both sides of the seat, parallel to the curve. Set the bevel on the bandsaw and cut out the seat. With your router and a ³/₈-inch round-over bit, round off the fore-and-aft corners of the seat (you can do this with your plane and sandpaper if you don't have a router). Smooth the ends with your block plane and round the upper corners of the ends ¹/₈ inch.

8. Now locate the post for the rowing version. Draw a centerline on the bottom of the boat under the seat location. With a square, from the seat, locate the width of the seat on the centerline. Find the center of the seat along the centerline. If this mark puts the post on a plank seam, adjust it one way or other so it doesn't land on the seam.

9. Remove the seat. Set the post over this location (either a 1¹/₂-inch square post — chamfered or rounded — or a turned post). Mark around the post onto the bottom planking so you can find the same position later.

10. Place a straightedge on the risers, across the boat, and mark where it crosses the post both fore and aft. Add ¹/₄ inch to these lines and cut the post to length.

11. Sand the post, drill, countersink, and fasten it with a screw on two sides, driven diagonally into the bottom.

12. Lay the seat over the post and screw it to the risers. Put a screw through the seat into the post. These screws should be countersunk just enough to be flush with the seat for easy removal.

Step H: Fit the guardrails.

1. Cut and shape the rail according to Figure 39.

2. Bevel the forward end of the rail to fit against the side of the outer stem.

Step I: Fit the knees for the center bench seat (make two).

The seat knees, which are screwed into the forward side of the center frame, give the boat additional strength and stiffness (see Figure 39). The leg of the knee that rests on the bench seat should be at least 10 inches long; the leg that is attached to the side of the boat runs from the seat to the sheer. The grain of the wood should run diagonally across the knee to insure maximum strength.

1. First make a pattern for the knees. The ability to fashion well-shaped knees helps the artistic boatbuilder stand out from the pack, so take your time and design carefully. You will be putting a screw through the rail into the knee; shape the top of the knee with enough wood so the screw will not split the knee. I like to leave about 1 inch here.

2. Check your pattern to insure it fits tightly at the side and on the seat, then lay it out on the knee stock, taking care to align the grain properly (see Figure 39). Do not cut the inside curve yet. You will want to fit the side and the seat edges first, so leave enough stock to cut the curve later. Both of the fitted edges may require beveling; check carefully and, if necessary, use your bevel gauge to take off the bevels. You should be an old hand at this by now!

3. When the knee fits, go ahead and cut the inside curve. Then smooth the curve with a half-round file followed by sandpaper. Take your time; we want no lumps here!

4. Place the knee in position and mark its footprint on the seat. Drill pilot holes and temporarily fasten as shown in Figure 39. When you are satisfied with the fit, remove the fastenings, bed the knee in flexible compound, and refasten.

Step J: Fit the oarlock pads (see Figure 39).

1. The oarlock pads must be designed to suit the oarlock sockets you purchased. The pad extends 1 inch above the rail and 1½ inches on each side of the oarlock socket. From the top down, the pad should measure at least 4 inches. It is fastened with two screws driven in through the planking at the bottom, and with two screws driven through the rail and the planking into the pad at the top.

2. There are two types of socket that I like for this boat. One, the Davis oarlock socket, allows the oarlock to be lifted and swung down from the rowing position and is manufactured as a single unit. The second type, for which oarlocks and sockets are sold separately, is illustrated in Figure 39.

Step K: Fit the brass half-oval stem and skeg bands.

1. I like to put a band of ⅝-inch brass half oval on the stem and along the skeg for protection against the dings and dents caused when the boat bumps a dock or drags on a rocky beach. In my area, I get ⅝-inch brass half-oval stock in 6-foot lengths from a supplier of brass and copper sheet, pipe, and other products. Many chandlers can order suitable stock, too.

2. I fasten 2 feet of this stock on the outer face of the stem, allowing approximately 4 inches to 5 inches extra to be bent under the heel of the stem and onto the keel. At the top I grind an arrowhead or round it off nicely. After grinding, use your finish sander with 100-grit paper, then 220-grit, followed by 600-grit to polish it up. More half oval is fastened on the skeg, allowing an extra 6 inches to be bent over onto the transom. Once again, finish off the ends.

3. The half oval comes undrilled, so you must drill holes through it at 6-inch intervals, closer near the bends. You can buy a star bit or similar device from a hardware store for forming the countersinks for the screw heads after the holes have been drilled.

4. The best fastenings for brass half oval are 1-inch #6 oval-head screws, but in a pinch 1-inch #8 flatheads will work, too. File the screw heads flush with the half oval after they have been driven.

IX

Filling, Painting, and Varnishing

Many years ago, I owned a 14-foot sailboat that I used nearly every day. I spent hours painting and varnishing every year, and the boat always gleamed. She was kept uncovered in the California sun, partly because covers cost too much and partly because of the owner's vanity. I spent a lot of time working on that boat, and I was constantly trying to improve my finishing skills. I therefore sought the best opinions available.

The advice that called the loudest was the simplest and the most profound; it was given to me by an old mariner. "Read the Can!" he said.

Is it really that simple? Yes, it is. In fact it is doubly so, as the paint companies keep developing new formulas that don't act like the enamel paint and varnishes that were once common. Many house paints are now designed for one-coat coverage, and clear coats are now made of many things besides varnish. I have experimented a bit with modern finishes, but for clear coats I have returned to using spar varnish, as it is the simplest and easiest to apply and I know I will get good service from it. I will provide advice here on that and other finishes, but first an old-time recipe for sealing and finishing the inside of the bottom:

This is homemade deck oil, which is a mixture of kerosene (approximately 20 percent of the total), boiled linseed oil, and pine tar (just plop in a shot of it to suit yourself). Everybody has their favorite mix, so experiment and develop your own. The concoction is heated — outside for safety, as there is danger of fumes and fire — and poured on the inside bottom of the boat, then rubbed around with rags or a paint brush that can hold up to hot oil. The kerosene drives the boiled linseed oil and pine tar into the wood, making it one of the best sealers ever.

Deck oil is all the finish necessary for the inside bottom of the boat. While it is not what you could call a "fine" finish, it is durable and very easy to renew; you will be stomping around on the bottom, anyway, and paint will always look scuffed and chipped. It will not work for the plywood bottom, however. This you will have to paint.

Keep in mind that there are as many finishing methods and philosophies as there are finishers. I offer you the benefit of my experience, but don't hesitate to consult your own experts.

To paint or to varnish?

That is the question. If you wish to minimize maintenance, paint the whole boat. A tasteful choice of colors and good workmanship will make it a work of art, just like a well-painted Victorian house.

When you look at the beautiful wood in your boat, you may change your mind and decide to use varnish to show it off. Before you make your decision, first take my varnish test, then read the section on what it takes to maintain a varnish finish. And keep in mind that a well-kept varnish finish is a glory to behold; a poorly maintained varnish finish is a real dog!

If you are still inclined to varnish, then have at it.

My varnish test: Do you wash and wax your car every week? Are you somewhat of a clean freak? Does the word finicky describe you? Do you have lots of spare time? If the answer is yes to all these questions, then go ahead and varnish. If you answered no and therefore flunked the varnish test, but you still can't resist the glories of a varnish finish, then consider a compromise: varnish only the guardrails and the outside of the transom, especially if you used Honduras mahogany for those parts.

By the way, the best way to preserve varnish is to keep the boat covered, as it is the sun's ultraviolet rays that break down the finish. The drawback to this method is that wooden boats don't do well if they are kept under hot covers, especially if they are poorly ventilated.

Prep work

Step one in finishing your boat is to fix any hammer marks or dings. Do this with boiling water. Just dab it on with a piece of terrycloth toweling. In a pinch just pour a little water on the blemish, right out of the pot. If more finesse is required, put wet toweling over the spot and apply heat with a soldering iron. The wood will swell and, in most cases, the dings and dents will disappear.

The next step is to fill the countersunk screws. If you are varnishing the rail and transom, the best practice is to fill the holes with bungs (plugs) cut from the same material as the underlying part. As you will have used a ⅜-inch drill countersink for the holes, a ⅜ plug cutter, used in a drill press, will quickly make the bungs. Alternatively, you could have a boatshop cut them for you, or purchase them ready-made from a chandler (boat supply store). If your countersunk hole is not deep enough to hold a bung, remove the screw and re-drill. When seating a bung in the hole, make sure the grain is running in the same direction as that of the underlying wood.

That will take care of the big holes. Now it's time to go to work with plastic wood putty, the same material used by cabinet workers; it is available at any hardware store. Apply with a putty knife and sand smooth after it has hardened. As previously mentioned, do not fill the holes in the removable seats.

When all the holes and blemishes are filled, clean up any excess putty, bedding compound, or adhesive, and lightly sand the boat. Sand over hard corners about ⅛ inch.

Varnish

I prefer to apply varnish first on a boat that will have both painted and varnished surfaces. If the paint is applied first, it is liable to spatter the bare wood that is to be varnished and ruin my careful preparation. When the paint is applied last, it is easy to wipe any errant paint off the cured varnish.

There are several types of varnish on the market. Talk to the people at the chandlery about the type that best stands up to the climate in your area. Whatever the type, however, be sure that it is formulated for marine use. Such varnish contains ultraviolet shields that will provide longer life in direct sunlight.

Polyurethane, which is a synthetic clear coat, can be used, but there are differences between it and varnish. If neglected, varnish can be brought back with new coats as long as peeling has not begun. Polyurethane is a plastic and, if let go, will become weak and opaque. If that happens, there is nothing for it but to strip the damaged finish to the bare wood and start again. From experience and from what I hear from others, I prefer varnish to polyurethane for exterior use.

But remember the varnish test. You should be prepared to apply several coats during the season to keep your finish bright.

To put down a proper varnish finish, you must first carefully sand the surface. When sanding by hand, sand only with the grain. Even the most minute strokes across the grain will reveal ugly scratches when varnished. An orbital sander works fine here.

Brushes should be new and made of high-quality China bristle or the equivalent. They should be cleaned scrupulously after use, and kept wrapped. Do not allow your brush to dry out. Many finishers, when working on a job that will take many days, store their brushes suspended in kerosene overnight to keep them from drying out and collecting dirt and dust.

Sanding sealers are not necessary for a varnished surface, but they can be used. They are useful, because they stiffen up the little feathers of wood left behind by the sander and allow you to easily sand them off. Most sealers are fast drying. Choose a sealer that is recommended by the varnish manufacturer. Mixing brands of sealers, varnish, and thinners can lead to the failure of the varnish and the ruination of your finish. Read the can!

The tried and true method of sealing is with a first coat of varnish thinned 10 percent with turpentine or mineral spirits. This coat must be sanded thoroughly, but the wood feathers, mentioned above, will make the job more difficult than if a sanding sealer were used.

I use fast sanding sealer to harden up softwoods, such as cedar and spruce, as soon as I have finished sanding or shaping. These woods easily collect dents, dings, smudges, and dirt as the boat is being built. The use of sealer will cut down the effects of this.

No matter how you seal the wood, the next coat is varnish, laid on full strength. There is usually little thinning required when varnishing. Care should be taken that the varnish is kept at the same temperature as the area where you will apply it. If it is kept at a cooler temperature, it might thin suddenly when applied, causing uncontrollable runs.

There is a technique for dealing with runs in varnish; it applies to paint, also. After a few minutes the coating will begin to cure; any attempts to brush out runs after this will cause drag marks. Instead, take a length of masking tape, one end in each hand, and lightly touch it to the run. The tape will lift it off. If the varnish has not yet begun to cure, the remaining varnish on the surface will lie down and no evidence of the run will remain. But if a mark is left in the varnish, don't fool with it. Rather, sand it out after the varnish has cured.

The first two to four coats of varnish seal and smooth the surface of the wood. On hardwoods, a fair amount of sanding between coats is required to create a smooth surface by the fourth coat. Softwoods usually become smooth by the second coat. Use a tack rag — a sticky cloth wipe available at paint stores — or a cloth soaked in paint thinner to clean up the surface between coats. Wet-or-dry sandpaper, 150-grit, is best for sanding the early coats. Use water with this sandpaper to keep the grits from clogging with newly cured varnish. Switch to 220-grit wet-or-dry for the third and fourth coats.

Most professional finishers feel there should be a minimum of four coats of varnish on new wood and six are even better. Count on adding at least two maintenance coats during the season, and starting off the new season next year with two more.

Work cleanly, carefully, and above all else, Read the Can!

Paint

Paint should be a high-quality exterior enamel. Chandlers carry the popular marine brands, but a house paint will work here, also.

Painted areas require sealing, and for this use primer thinned to the maximum recommended by the manufacturer. Then use a painter's glazing putty applied with a putty knife to fill any leftover dings. Larger holes or dents can be filled with auto body filler, but be sure to use the waterproof type.

When using glazing putty, take only a small amount out of the can at a time to insure that you apply only fresh putty and that the unused material doesn't start to cure. Store the can upside down.

Putties and fillers, if applied carefully and smoothly, will not require much sanding. When they are dry, sand the surface, then apply a second coat of thinned primer.

Primer is the most important part of a good finish. Most finish coats are designed to lay down, giving you a smooth finish. Any imperfections in the primer coat, such as brush stroke marks, will show through the finish coats. Therefore, carefully sand out brush strokes in the primer with 150-grit, then 220-grit wet-or-dry sandpaper, and, if necessary, apply a third coat of primer.

Be especially careful not to sand through sharp corners. Sand-through areas will appear as dark splotches in the finish coats. Many high-quality enamel finishes are not very opaque and will continue to show the dark marks of the sand-through areas even after several coats. This is why I prefer to use high-quality exterior enamel house paint over marine enamel. House paints are designed to cover in one coat, and therefore are rich with opaque solids. This makes them more forgiving than the enamels that are sold in the marine stores. I also prefer satin-finish paint to high gloss, as it obscures primer brush strokes, dents, and other imperfections, and is easy to repair.

If you are painting the boat with several colors, determine in advance the order of application and mask off areas that are to be painted later. Two coats of each finish color should do it.

X

A Good Pair of Oars

A good pair of oars is hard to find and therefore best made by you. Oar building is a pleasurable experience, and the result, a lightweight, well-designed oar, is a joy to behold and use.

Sitka spruce is the favorite material for oars here in the Northwest, though I have used old-growth fir selected for even grain and light weight. Clear, vertical-grain stock is best. In the East, ash and native spruce have been used for oars. Basswood can also be used in a pinch.

In the past I was able to find good oar-making material at lumberyards by carefully examining the wood in the stacks. This has become nearly impossible of late, as it is now the practice in the Northwest to use trees of small diameter for house construction lumber. However, things change, and in your area this method might still work. Check your local sources.

Oars come in all shapes and sizes. Some have straight blades; some curved or spoon shaped. All designs are attempts to maximize the small amount of horsepower, approximately ¼ hp, the human body can develop. Competitive rowers use spoon-bladed oars, sliding seats, and outrig-gers to improve this output, but for plain, old-fashioned recreational rowing in a fixed seat, I like the straight-bladed oar best. The limited fore-and-aft body motion that the fixed seat allows doesn't give much advantage to a spoon oar. Besides, people who use their boats around docks and harbors are likely to want to push off with the tip of the blade, a practice that can be the ruination of a delicate spoon oar.

Besides shape, the width of the blade is a variable. Think of blade width roughly in terms of the gearing of a bicycle; the wider the blade, the lower the gear. Heavy boats encourage a narrow blade. The down side is that a narrow blade requires more strokes per minute to deliver the same amount of power as a wide blade. The narrower the blade, the more strokes.

The oar we will make here is a time-tested, general-purpose design that will produce a simple and effective oar (see Figure 40). The oar is 8 feet long, with a 5-inch-wide blade; it is constructed of stock with a finished dimension of 1¾ inches by 1¾ inches. If you look at Figure 41, you can see that in profile, to maintain its strength, the shaft maintains its 1¾-inch dimension all the way from the handle to the neck. In the top view the oar tapers from the leather area to the neck. Here are the construction steps:

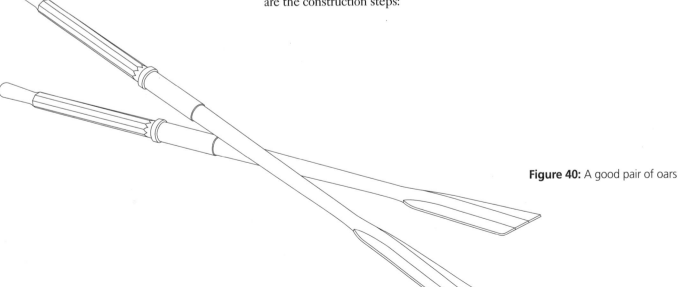

Figure 40: A good pair of oars

65

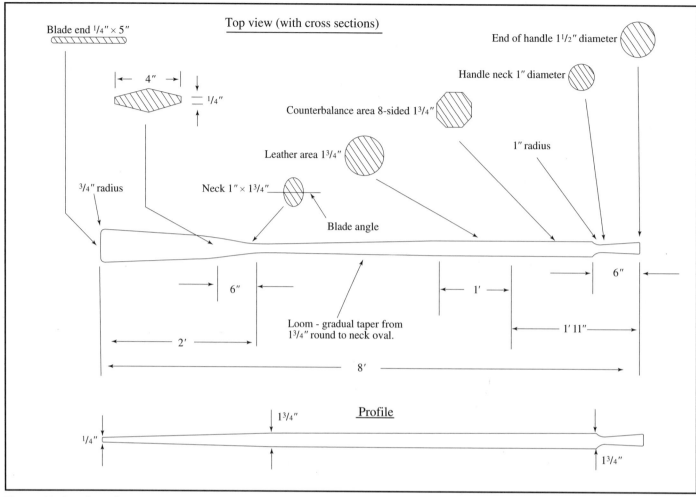

Top view (with cross sections)

Blade end $^{1}/_{4}'' \times 5''$

End of handle $1^{1}/_{2}''$ diameter

4″

$^{1}/_{4}''$

Handle neck 1″ diameter

Counterbalance area 8-sided $1^{3}/_{4}''$

Leather area $1^{3}/_{4}''$

1″ radius

$^{3}/_{4}''$ radius

Neck $1'' \times 1^{3}/_{4}''$

Blade angle

6″

1′

6″

Loom - gradual taper from $1^{3}/_{4}''$ round to neck oval.

2′

1′ 11″

8′

Profile

$1^{3}/_{4}''$

$^{1}/_{4}''$

$1^{3}/_{4}''$

Figure 41: Oar dimensions

1. Mark the profile on the oar stock (see Figure 42). The taper begins 2 feet from the tip end of the blade. The tip is ¼ inch thick. Cut this out.

2. Make a poster board pattern of one-half of the handle. Mark the handle on the profile. Cut the profile on the bandsaw.

3. Cut the blade taper on two 2-foot long pieces of 1¾-inch by 1¾-inch oar stock and glue up the oar blank (see Figure 43).

4. Mark the handle on the top side of the oar blank. Mark the neck width and the two blade widths as shown. Then mark the beginning and the end of the counterbalance and leather areas. To determine the loom taper, hold your batten along one edge of the oar blank at the counterbalance and the leather areas. The oar siding is parallel in these areas. Bend the batten until it touches the mark at the neck. The batten's slight bend will determine the taper of the loom. Mark this taper and connect the marks. The tapers need not be of rocket-science caliber. Use your imagination. The lines should all blend into each other smoothly. When you like the looks of this line, duplicate it on the other side.

5. Cut out the top view.

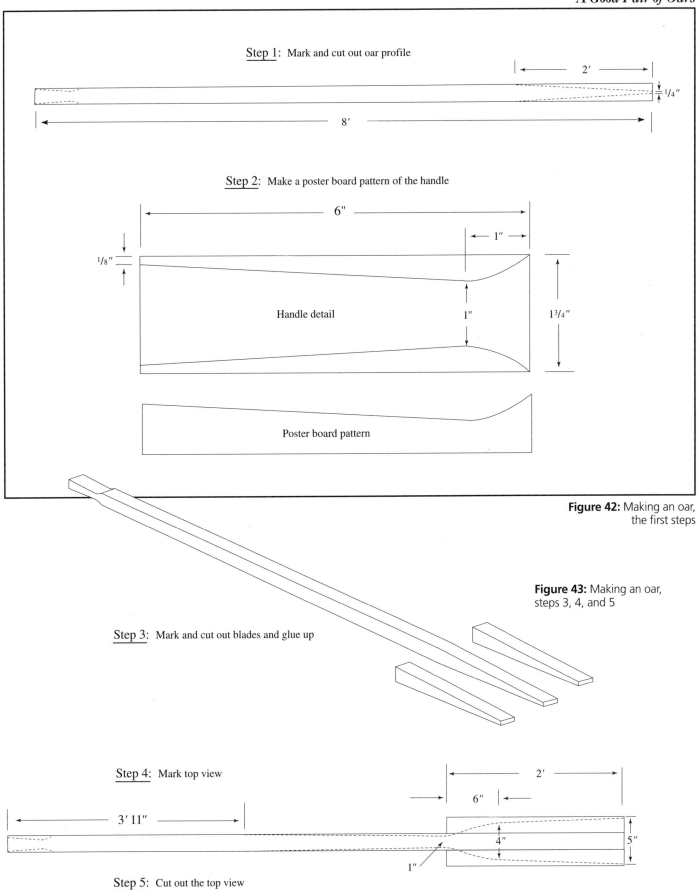

Step 1: Mark and cut out oar profile

2′

1/4″

8′

Step 2: Make a poster board pattern of the handle

6″

1″

1/8″

Handle detail

1″

1³/4″

Poster board pattern

Figure 42: Making an oar, the first steps

Figure 43: Making an oar, steps 3, 4, and 5

Step 3: Mark and cut out blades and glue up

Step 4: Mark top view

2′

6″

3′ 11″

4″

5″

1″

Step 5: Cut out the top view

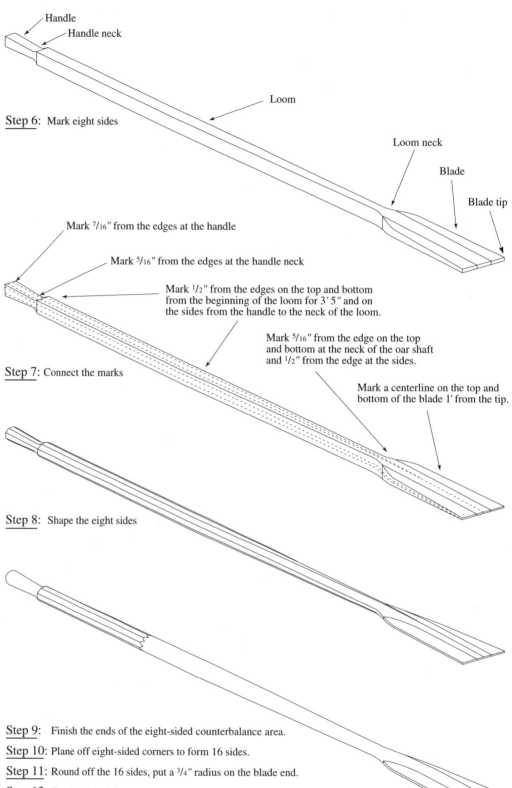

Step 6: Mark eight sides

Handle

Handle neck

Loom

Loom neck

Blade

Blade tip

Mark $7/16''$ from the edges at the handle

Mark $5/16''$ from the edges at the handle neck

Mark $1/2''$ from the edges on the top and bottom
from the beginning of the loom for 3' 5'' and on
the sides from the handle to the neck of the loom.

Mark $5/16''$ from the edge on the top
and bottom at the neck of the oar shaft
and $1/2''$ from the edge at the sides.

Mark a centerline on the top and
bottom of the blade 1' from the tip.

Step 7: Connect the marks

Step 8: Shape the eight sides

Figure 44: Making an oar,
steps 6, 7, 8, 9, 10, 11, 12, and 13

Step 9: Finish the ends of the eight-sided counterbalance area.

Step 10: Plane off eight-sided corners to form 16 sides.

Step 11: Round off the 16 sides, put a $3/4''$ radius on the blade end.

Step 12: Sand and seal the oar.

Step 13: Apply a minimum of 4 coats of varnish.

6. The shaft of the oar is eight-sided, then sixteen-
sided, and then rounded. To develop the eight
sides, mark the widths as shown in Figure 44.

7. Connect the marks.

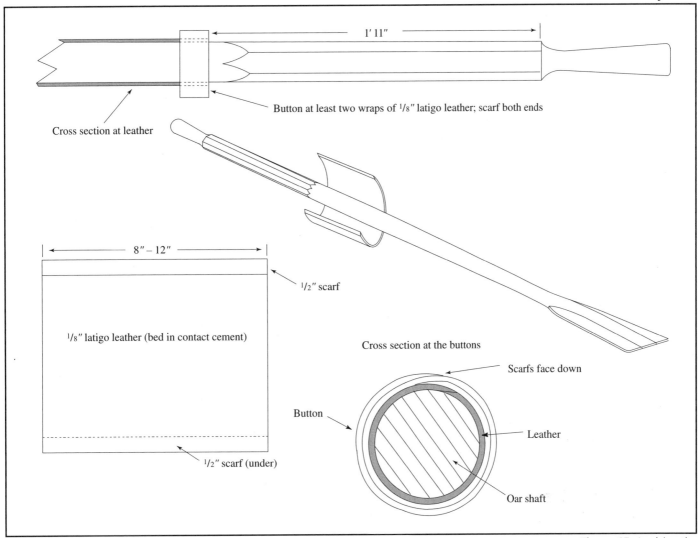

Cross section at leather

Button at least two wraps of ¹/₈″ latigo leather; scarf both ends

8″ – 12″

¹/₂″ scarf

¹/₈″ latigo leather (bed in contact cement)

¹/₂″ scarf (under)

Cross section at the buttons

Scarfs face down

Button

Leather

Oar shaft

Figure 45: Applying the leathers on the oars

8. Shape the eight sides. Take care to maintain all eight sides even in width.

9. Finish the ends of the counterbalance area, which will remain eight-sided in the finished oar.

10. By eye, plane the oars from the beginning of the leather to the neck to a 16-sided figure. Do this by taking one long plane stroke on each corner until all the flats are equal. Take your time here, and you will be rewarded by a beautifully faired oar.

11. With your block plane set fine, plane off the tiny flats. Take long overlapping strokes.

12. Fold a sheet of 80-grit sandpaper into thirds. Sand the oar round by taking long, overlapping strokes. Check with your hand for lumps. Eyeball the edges. If necessary, plane off any lumps with your block plane. Fold a sheet of 100-grit sandpaper into thirds and repeat the sanding process. Then go over the oar with 150-grit. Apply at least one coat of a sanding sealer. When the sealer dries, sand the oar smooth with 150-grit sandpaper.

13. Apply at least four coats of varnish.

Leather is used to wrap the part of the loom that rubs in the oarlock (see Figure 45). I obtain mine at a local tannery, where they recommend an oiled leather called "latigo" leather, which is about ⅛ inch thick. To feather the leather for a smooth outer surface, scarfs are cut at the ends with a sharp chisel. A belt sander can be used for this, too.

A 1-inch wide strip of leather called the button is wrapped twice around the leather once it has been applied to keep the oar from sliding through the oarlock if you let go of it. The buttons are tapered at the ends so they will lay fair without noticeable lumps.

The leathers are attached with contact cement right over the varnish. This is a simple and durable solution to the problem of attaching the leathers without resorting to nails, which weaken the oar. To hold the leather on the oar while the glue sets, wrap it with an old bicycle inner tube. There are fancier ways to fasten leathers, such as hand sewing the seam, but this is the simplest I have found.

Figure 46: Rigging plan

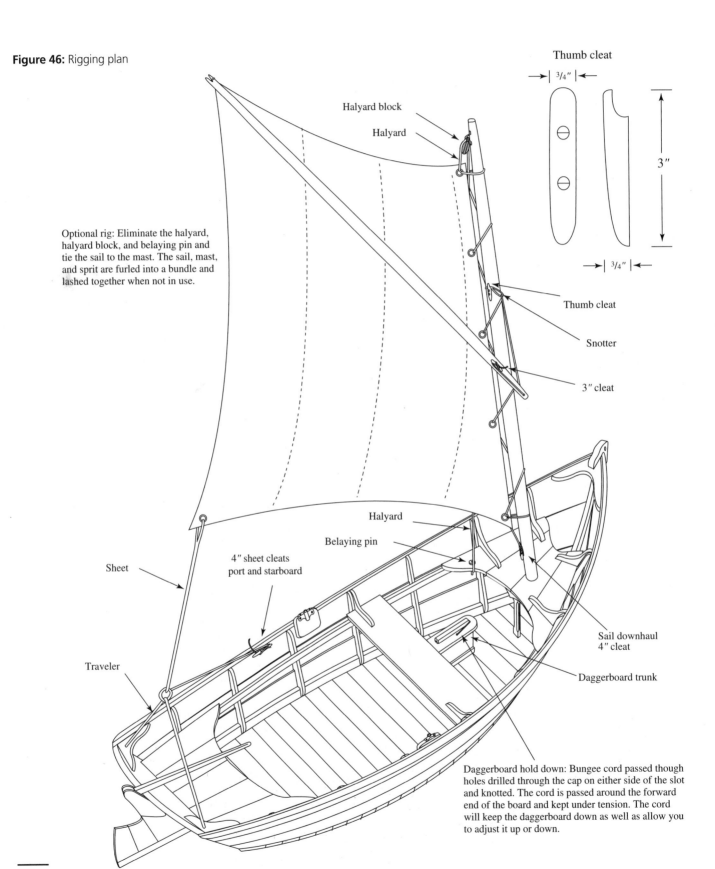

Thumb cleat

3/4″

3″

3/4″

Halyard block

Halyard

Optional rig: Eliminate the halyard, halyard block, and belaying pin and tie the sail to the mast. The sail, mast, and sprit are furled into a bundle and lashed together when not in use.

Thumb cleat

Snotter

3″ cleat

Halyard

Belaying pin

4″ sheet cleats port and starboard

Sheet

Traveler

Sail downhaul 4″ cleat

Daggerboard trunk

Daggerboard hold down: Bungee cord passed though holes drilled through the cap on either side of the slot and knotted. The cord is passed around the forward end of the board and kept under tension. The cord will keep the daggerboard down as well as allow you to adjust it up or down.

XI

The Sailing Rig

A simple, well-designed skiff is a versatile craft. It does nearly everything well, including sailing. A sprit rig is a simple sail plan that has been successfully used on skiffs for generations (see Figures 46 and 47), so we will use it here. I will show you how to rig the sail with a halyard to hoist it and a belaying pin to tie the halyard to, an arrangement that allows you to take the sail down when you want to row without removing the mast. Having the halyard tied off to the pin through the seat also prevents the mast from jumping out of the step in rough water.

As I wrote these words an old friend reminded me that many people might prefer to do away with the halyard and the belaying pin, and simply tie the sail to the mast. With an arrangement like this, to remove the sail, all you have to do is roll the sail around the mast, with the sprit inside, wrap the entire mess with a simple lashing, and pull out the mast. There are no fittings on the mast, only a ⅝-inch hole through the top of the mast. This is as simple as it gets! So I offer this rig as an alternative.

Sailing craft require a keel or centerboard of some sort to counteract leeway, or the tendency of the wind to push the boat sideways. Our choices are among a leeboard, which is an adjustable plank attached to the outside of the boat; a centerboard, which is a pivoting plank permanently housed in a long trunk on the centerline of the boat; and a daggerboard, which is a removable plank passed vertically through a narrow trunk on the centerline of the boat. I prefer a daggerboard for small boats like this, as it is simple, lightweight, and easy to build.

To adapt this skiff for a sailing rig, we will strengthen the forward seat with knees and mast partners, and cut a hole for the mast (see Figures 47 and 48). A maststep is placed under the seat. A daggerboard trunk is constructed and fastened over a slot cut through the bottom of the boat. A daggerboard, rudder, and tiller are built, and the mast and sprit are shaped.

Materials required

Mast — spruce, fir, or basswood, 2½ inches by 2½ inches by 11 feet long.

Sprit — fir or spruce, ¾ inches by 1½ inches by 11 feet long.

Partners, knees, daggerboard, rudder, tiller — Honduras mahogany or fir, ¾ inch by 8 inches by 14 feet long.

Step A: Fit the forward seat.

1. The forward seat is constructed the same way as described in Chapter 8 for the rowing version, except that two mast partners, ¾ inch by 6 inches wide, are added (see Figure 48) and a 3-inch mast hole is cut.

2. To locate the hole, remove the forward seat planks. With poster board, make a pattern of the area outlined by the forward and after seat frames and the risers (see Figure 49). To do this, place the poster board so it overlaps the framing and the risers, and mark the shape from underneath. Cut this out and check the fit, which should be exact.

3. On this pattern, draw a line parallel to the after frame, half the distance between the forward and the after frames. This line marks the seam between the two mast partners.

4. The mast partners will be beveled at the ends to fit tightly to the risers on each side. The seat planks will be screwed into the partners, creating a strong structure for supporting the mast (see Figures 48 and 49). To determine the bevels, lay a plank across the risers midway between the forward and after seat frame. With your bevel gauge held vertically, 90 degrees to the riser, measure the bevel at both risers (this is done in the event the bevels are different, which is possible).

5. Make sure that one edge of the partner stock is planed straight and true. Place the pattern over the partner stock, with the centerline at one edge. Mark the shape of the plank. Set the proper bevel on your bandsaw or sabersaw and cut it out. Do the same with the second partner. Fit the partners into the risers and plane the partners to fit. There is no need to get carried away here. Make the fit as best you can, as the partners can be bedded in flexible compound, which will make up for any variations.

Figure 47: Sail plan

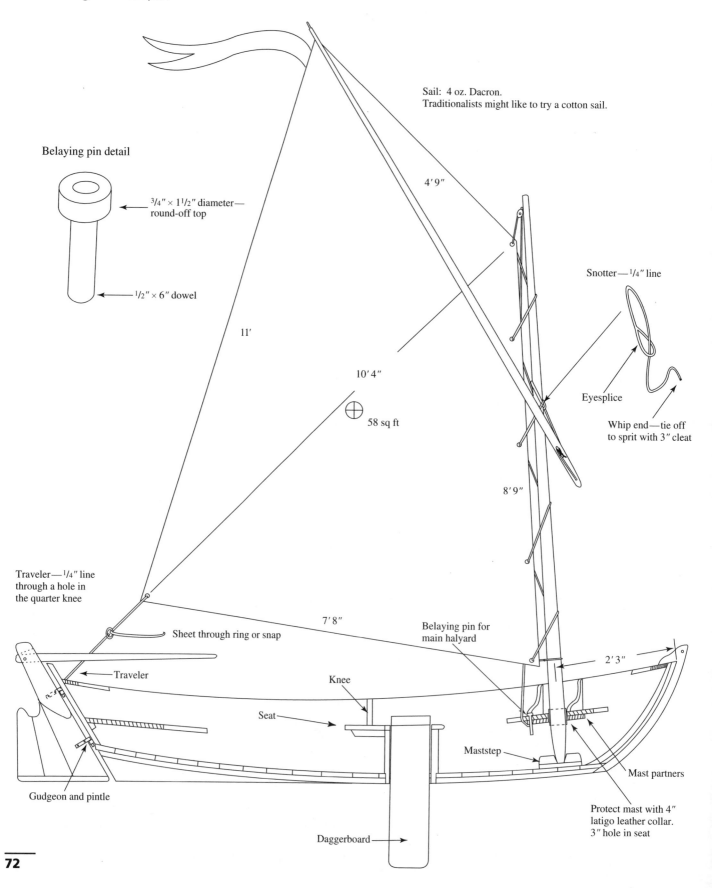

Sail: 4 oz. Dacron.
Traditionalists might like to try a cotton sail.

4' 9"

Belaying pin detail

3/4" × 1 1/2" diameter—
round-off top

1/2" × 6" dowel

Snotter—1/4" line

Eyesplice

Whip end—tie off
to sprit with 3" cleat

11'

10' 4"

⊕

58 sq ft

8' 9"

Traveler—1/4" line
through a hole in
the quarter knee

Sheet through ring or snap

7' 8"

Belaying pin for
main halyard

2' 3"

Traveler

Knee

Seat

Maststep

Mast partners

Gudgeon and pintle

Protect mast with 4"
latigo leather collar.
3" hole in seat

Daggerboard

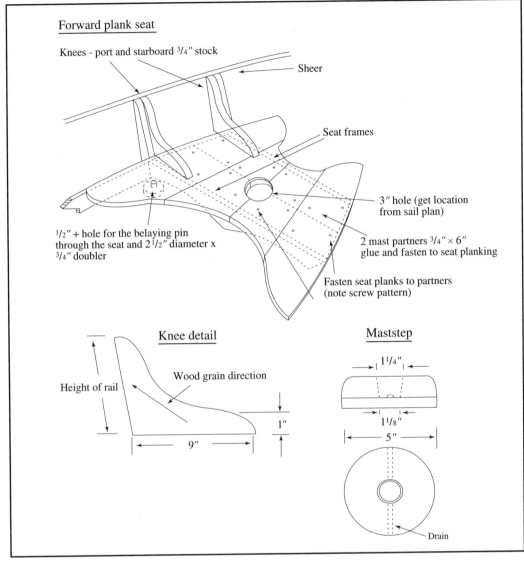

Forward plank seat

Knees - port and starboard ³/₄″ stock

Sheer

Seat frames

3″ hole (get location from sail plan)

¹/₂″ + hole for the belaying pin through the seat and 2¹/₂″ diameter x ³/₄″ doubler

2 mast partners ³/₄″ × 6″ glue and fasten to seat planking

Fasten seat planks to partners (note screw pattern)

Knee detail

Height of rail

Wood grain direction

9″

1″

Maststep

1¹/₄″

1¹/₈″

5″

Drain

Figure 48:
Mast partners, knees, and step

6. Fasten one side of the seat in place, and screw it to the partners. Mark the location of the seam between the partners on the top of the seat. Then refasten the other side of the seat and fasten it to the partners. Follow the screw pattern shown in Figure 48. Be sure to keep screws out of a 3-inch-diameter area around the mark you made above. Do not screw in the seat permanently until you have fastened in the maststep.

7. With a 3-inch hole saw, drill the mast hole, centered on the mark you made. In a pinch, you can use your sabersaw to cut this hole; for a starter hole, first use a ³/₄-inch paddle bit in your drill.

8. The maststep is made of a 5-inch diameter base of ³/₄-inch stock and an upper piece of 1¹/₂-inch stock (see Figure 48). A 1¹/₈-inch hole is drilled through the center of the upper piece and opened with a file to 1¹/₄ inch at the top, creating a tapered hole. On the bottom of the top piece, a channel is chiseled. When the top is joined with the base, the channel will act as a water drain.

9. To locate the position of the maststep, make sure the boat is sitting directly on the floor. Wedge up under the side of the bottom, so the boat is level when measured athwartships (from side to side). Place a stick of wood, 1¹/₂ inches by ³/₄ inch by 11 feet (the stock for the sprit should work fine), in the mast hole. It should rest on the bottom of the boat. Use your level to ensure the straightedge is plumb. Using this straightedge as your guide, extend the center of the mast hole to the bottom of the boat on the centerline, and mark it. Make another mark ¹/₂ inch forward of this point, also on the centerline. This is the center of the maststep.

10. Remove the seat and the mast partners. Center the maststep over the point determined above and screw it down temporarily with 3-inch #12 bronze or stainless-steel screws.

11. When you are satisfied with the fit, remove the maststep, bed it in flexible compound, and refasten it permanently. Do the same with the mast partners and the seat.

Step 1:
Make a pattern of the area within the risers and seat frames. Locate a line centered between the forward and after seat frames and mark the 3″ diameter mast hole location.

Step 2:
Cut out mast partners from 6″ stock. Take off bevel at the risers.

Bevel the partners to fit tightly to risers

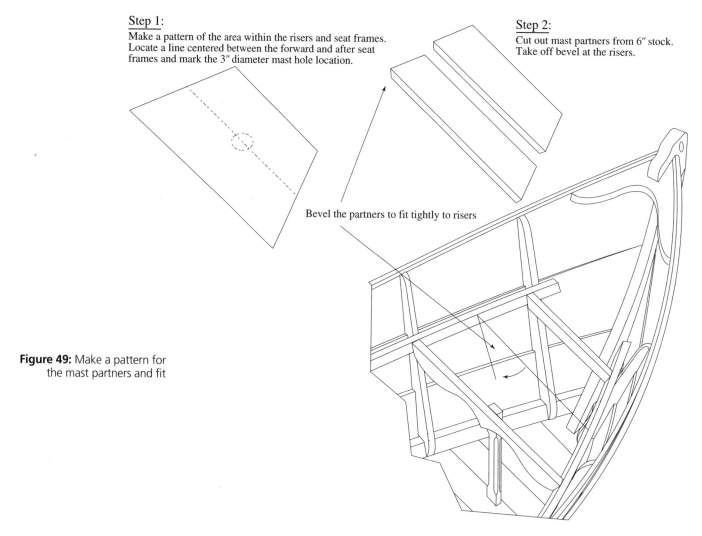

Figure 49: Make a pattern for the mast partners and fit

Step B: Fit the forward seat knees.

1. The forward seat knees are similar to the center seat knees (see Figures 46 and 47). There will be four in all, two to a side. Take care in designing these knees; their shape should be consistent with that of the center knees. The foot of each knee is 9 inches long, and the side arm runs from the seat to the sheer. Make a pattern using the pattern from the center seat knees as a guide for the curved inner edge.

2. Using the pattern, cut and adjust the fit of the knees as you did for the center seat knees. Be sure that the bottom of the knees is beveled to fit tightly to the seat.

3. Locate the two knees against the forward side of Frame 2, port and starboard (see Figure 48), and fasten them as you did the center seat. Then repeat the process for the two knees on the after side of Frame 1.

Step C: Fit the belaying pin.

1. The belaying pin performs two functions. First, it provides a place to tie off the sail halyard. Second, it holds the mast down into the maststep. Without the security provided by the pin, the mast might jump out of the step, so don't leave it out.

2. Basically the pin is a ½-inch dowel fitted in a hole drilled through the seat (see Figures 47 and 48). Back up the hole with a doubler. With a round file, open the hole so the dowel will not freeze in the hole when the wood swells.

3. There is a round cap on the dowel to keep it from slipping through the hole. You can make your own with a hole saw, or use a maple knob, drilled to fit, from the hardware store. Here is another place where you can exercise your imagination.

4. The halyard is tied by bringing it down around the pin under the seat, then brought over the front of the seat and wrapped around the halyard. Do this several times, and tie off with a half hitch. It sounds more complicated than it is.

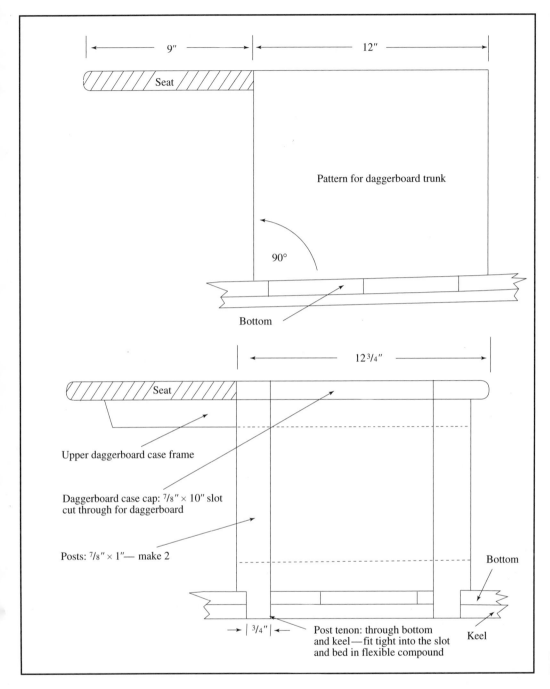

Figure 50:
Daggerboard trunk profile

Step D: Fit the daggerboard trunk.

1. The daggerboard trunk sides are made of ½-inch plank, or ⅜-inch plywood if you prefer; the framing is of ⅞-inch by 1-inch stock (fir or Honduras mahogany is preferred). A cap is placed over the trunk with a slot cut to accommodate the daggerboard.

2. The first step is to determine the shape of the trunk sides. We do this by first cutting out the framing for the top of the trunk. For the top frames, cut two pieces 18 inches long. You can finish off one end at an angle (see Figure 50).

3. The bottom of the trunk is curved slightly to fit the bottom. The after bottom corner of the daggerboard trunk is 90 degrees to the bottom. Place a combination square fore and aft on the bottom centerline in front of the seat. Move it aft until it touches the forward edge of the seat. Mark the point where the square hits the bottom.

4. Now turn the square 90 degrees, keeping it lined up on the point you marked on the bottom. Mark where the square hits the seat. This is the centerline of the daggerboard. Clamp one of the top frames to the underside of the seat at this centerline. The frame will extend 12 inches forward of the seat. The frame should be square to the seat.

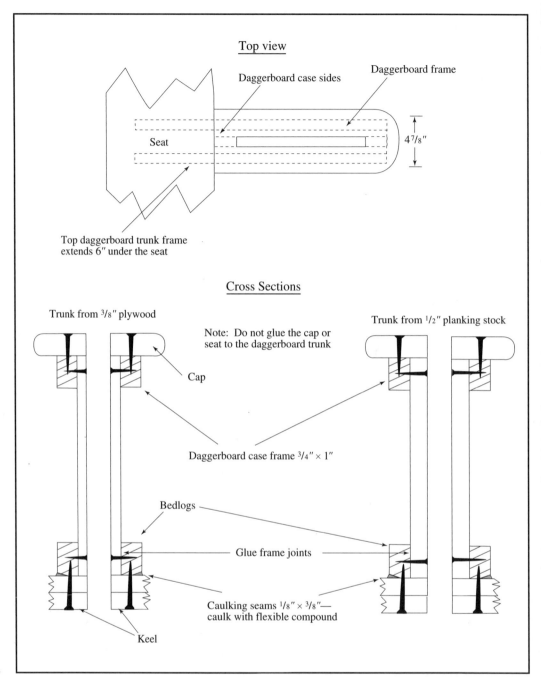

Top view

Daggerboard case sides

Daggerboard frame

Seat

4⁷/₈″

Top daggerboard trunk frame
extends 6″ under the seat

Cross Sections

Trunk from ³/₈″ plywood

Trunk from ¹/₂″ planking stock

Note: Do not glue the cap or
seat to the daggerboard trunk

Cap

Daggerboard case frame ³/₄″ × 1″

Bedlogs

Glue frame joints

Caulking seams ¹/₈″ × ³/₈″—
caulk with flexible compound

Keel

Figure 51: Daggerboard cap and
daggerboard trunk cross sections

5. The side of the trunk will fit tightly on the bottom and overlap the top frame. Get out a piece of poster board, 12 inches wide and high enough to reach from the bottom to a few inches over the frame. Clamp the poster board to the top frame so it touches the seat; the after edge must be square to the bottom and in line to the mark on the bottom. Push the pattern as close to the bottom as possible without losing square. This will probably leave a gap at the bottom (every boat is different). Set a pencil compass to the largest gap and, holding the compass vertically, move it along the pattern. Cut to this line and check the pattern to the bottom. If it fits, mark the top edge of the top frame on the pattern. Cut to this line. This is the shape of the daggerboard trunk sides.

6. Check this pattern against your planking stock. The grain of the stock should go fore and aft. If you don't have enough width in your stock, you can edge-glue an extra piece of stock to the top of the trunk. Fit the edges tightly, and glue with epoxy. With your pattern, mark the stock and cut out the shape. Leave the top edge long by ¹/₂ inch until you are sure the bottom fits tightly. Then put each side against the top frame. If the bottom fits, mark the side at the top of the frame and cut it out. Plane the edges smooth. (If you use plywood for the trunk sides, the process is the same.)

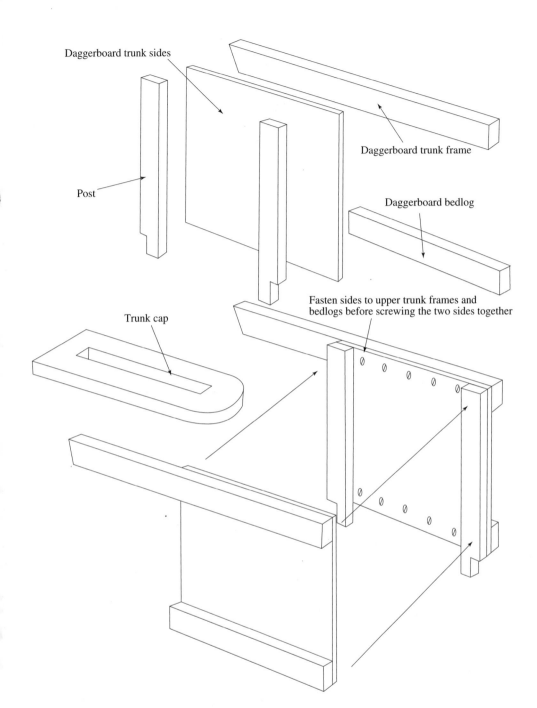

Daggerboard trunk sides

Daggerboard trunk frame

Post

Daggerboard bedlog

Fasten sides to upper trunk frames and bedlogs before screwing the two sides together

Trunk cap

Figure 52: Exploded view of daggerboard assembly

7. The bedlogs (bottom frames) are placed along the bottom of the trunk side, and the curve of the trunk bottom is marked on their lower edges and cut. Cut a caulking seam ⅛ inch wide by ⅜ inch deep on the outside edge of each bottom frame (see Figure 51). Glue and screw the bottom frames to the outside of each side. Fasten through the planking and the keel into the bedlogs (see Figure 51).

8. Place both sides of the trunk in the boat and locate the top frames along the top of the side and under the seat. If all fits, fasten and glue the top frames to the outside of the trunk sides. Fasten through the trunk planking into the frames.

9. The vertical frames that hold the sides apart are called the posts, or the headledges. Lay the framing stock on the forward and after edges of the trunk sides, and mark the top and bottom. At the bottom we will cut a tenon that will extend through the bottom and the keel. The tenon is 1 inch and starts ¼ inch in from the outside edge of each post. Extend the inside line of the post 1½ inches past the line of the bottom. Draw a line parallel to it, 1 inch away. Cut to these lines (see Figure 52).

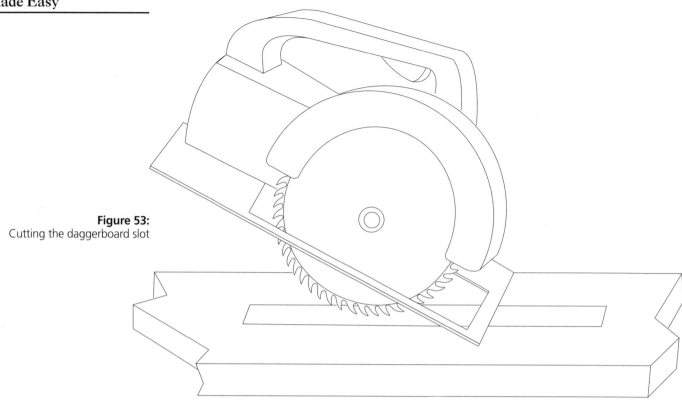

Figure 53:
Cutting the daggerboard slot

10. Clamp the pieces together and drill for screws, which will be used temporarily to hold the assembly together.

11. Now you must cut a slot in the bottom for the daggerboard. Place the daggerboard trunk in the boat and center it over the bottom centerline. Mark the footprint of the tenons on the bottom. Connect the footprints to outline the slot. Be sure that the slot measures ⅞ inch on the inside of the marks.

12. There are several ways to cut the slot. My favorite is to use a ¾-inch paddle drill bit to drill out the ends of the slot. Place a piece of wood under the hole to be drilled to prevent tearing as the paddle bit exits the hole. Then use a circular saw to plunge-cut the slot (see Figure 53). A sabersaw can also be used, although it is difficult to keep the line as straight as with the circular saw.

If you haven't plunge-cut with a circular saw before, practice on a piece of scrap clamped firmly to a sawhorse. Set the blade deep. Tilt the saw up on the forward edge of the guide, keeping the blade away from the bottom. Turn on the saw and slowly move it forward as you lower it, leaving the guidelines. Do not move the saw backward, as it will grab and destroy your work. You can turn it around and cut the other way to get the whole slot. Cut both sides on the inside of the line until you reach the drilled hole. Use a handsaw to finish the cut. A sharp chisel will square off the ends. Smooth out the sides of the slot with a file and a sanding block (sandpaper wrapped around a block of wood).

13. Fit the trunk over the slot and make a final check. Use epoxy to glue the daggerboard trunk parts together and refasten. Use long screws to go through the top and bottom frames, the planking, and the posts. Clean up quickly and thoroughly. Put the trunk back into the boat. Mark the footprint of the trunk by drawing a line around the trunk on the bottom. Fasten the top frame through the seat and the bottom frame through the keel. If all looks good, drill and drive temporary fastenings. To locate the bottom fastenings, drill pilot holes from the inside out on the bottom using the footprint as a guide. Then countersink and fasten from the outside. When you are satisfied, remove the temporary fastenings and refasten, using bedding compound on the bottom. Be sure to fill the caulking seams, and clean up thoroughly afterward.

14. The daggerboard cap fits over the top of the trunk and protrudes ¾ inch over the forward edge and sides. It should fit tightly against the forward side of the seat. Cut the slot as you did on the bottom, or make it up of two 2-inch pieces held apart by two ⅞-inch-wide pieces. Glue this assembly to the seat and centerboard trunk.

15. Round over the edges of the seat and the cap.

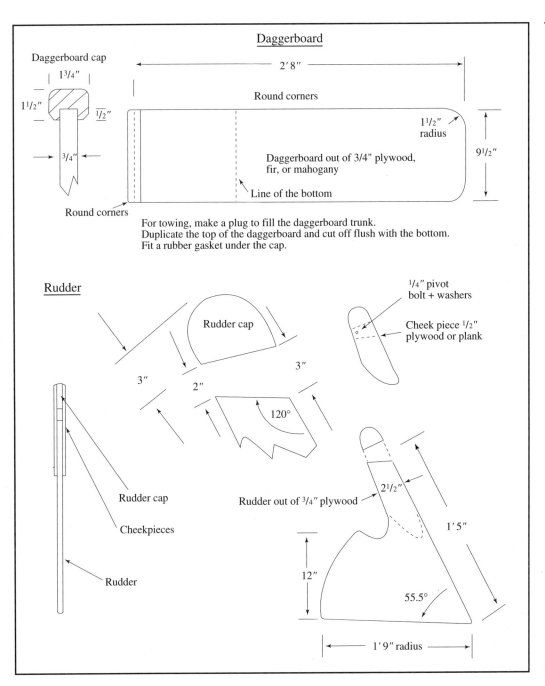

Figure 54: Daggerboard and rudder dimensions

Step E: Make the daggerboard.

1. The daggerboard is made from ¾-inch by 9 ½-inch stock (see Figure 54). I prefer vertical-grain fir for its stiffness and light weight, but ¾-inch marine plywood will also work fine. If you use plywood, lay out the plywood so the outside grain of the ply is running lengthwise. Racing sailors shape the edges of the daggerboard to an airfoil, but oldtimers maintain that this is not necessary, that simple rounding-off will do. If you decide on an airfoil shape, use solid wood; for rounding off, use solid lumber or plywood.

The daggerboard should extend ½ inch above the top of the trunk. As the top of the trunk is probably not square to the posts, cut the top of the board to match this angle. A cap is fitted over the top of the board; it is 1½ inches deep by 1¾ inches wide, rounded on the top and beveled on the bottom (see Figure 54).

2. If your skiff is to be towed behind a larger boat, make a plug for the daggerboard slot. This plug should reach through the trunk to the bottom and should have a tight-fitting cap at the top. This is an important piece of equipment, as without a plug, towing could force water up through the daggerboard trunk and fill the boat. A rubber gasket fitted tightly around the bottom of the handle will prevent water from getting into the boat.

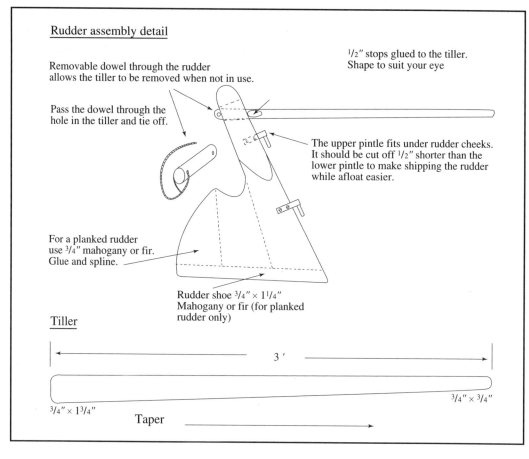

Rudder assembly detail

Removable dowel through the rudder
allows the tiller to be removed when not in use.

Pass the dowel through the
hole in the tiller and tie off.

$1/2''$ stops glued to the tiller.
Shape to suit your eye

The upper pintle fits under rudder cheeks.
It should be cut off $1/2''$ shorter than the
lower pintle to make shipping the rudder
while afloat easier.

For a planked rudder
use $3/4''$ mahogany or fir.
Glue and spline.

Rudder shoe $3/4'' \times 1^{1}/4''$
Mahogany or fir (for planked
rudder only)

Tiller

3 '

$3/4'' \times 1^{3}/4''$

Taper

$3/4'' \times 3/4''$

Figure 55:
Tiller and rudder detail

Step F: Make the rudder.

The rudder can be made of ¾-inch marine plywood or ¾-inch fir or mahogany planks. I have built my planked rudders using a glued-seam construction method for years. Old-timers might not trust the glue joints to hold against the pressure of swelling wood, but I have found that the rudder is not in the water long enough to swell much at all, as it is removed and stored away after each sail. If the rudder is used this way, and it is well sealed and painted, it should last for years.

In the event you would like to build your rudder the old way, here is how it is done:

The planks are pinned together with long brass or bronze pins hammered into holes drilled for a tight fit. A washer is placed over the pin; as hammering progresses, the end of the pin spreads to form a rim over the washer when the pin is all the way down.

Some boatbuilders thread the end of the pin and lay on a washer and a nut. When the pin is driven all the way home, they tighten the nut.

My method of choice is to spline and glue the rudder planks together, or to use plywood. No matter which method you use, simply round over the corners of the finished rudder; an airfoil shape is unnecessary.

1. First fit the gudgeons — the part of the rudder hinge with the hole — to the transom. The gudgeons, like the pintles — the part with the pin — are available in cast brass or bronze from most chandleries. The lower gudgeon is positioned approximately 1 inch above the bottom of the

boat, on the centerline, and the upper one goes at the height of the sheer.

2. If you are using ¾-inch plywood, draft the shape of the rudder right on the plywood and cut it out. The cheek pieces should be of ½-inch plywood or plank; they are glued and screwed to the sides of the rudder as shown in Figure 54. Before you glue the cheekpieces, however, first fit the top pintle. (More on the fitting of pintles below.) Then chisel the inside of the cheekpieces so they will fit over the upper pintle, and fit the rudder cap. Glue, screw, and round over.

3. The upper pintle should be made shorter than the lower one, which will make mounting the rudder easier when the boat is in the water. Cut off approximately ½ inch of the pintle's pin and round it over with a file.

The location of the pintles is determined by holding the rudder up against the boat, with the bottom of the rudder ½ inch above the bottom of the skeg. Mark the points where the top of the gudgeons touch the rudder, which is where the bottoms of the pintles must be aligned. Mount the pintles using through-bolts.

4. It is important to have a hold-down on the rudder (see Figure 55), as otherwise it will float off the boat. I suggest a simple hold-down consisting of a short length of bungee cord with a snap on the end, connecting the rudder to an eyestrap on the transom. There are plenty of other possible arrangements. Perhaps you can invent something even better!

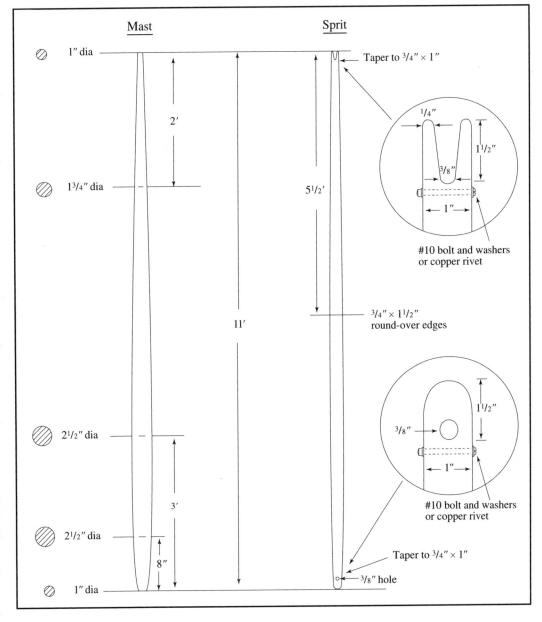

Mast

Sprit

1" dia

Taper to ³/₄" × 1"

2'

1/4"

1¹/₂"

³/₄" dia

5¹/₂'

³/₈"

1"

#10 bolt and washers
or copper rivet

³/₄" × 1¹/₂"
round-over edges

11'

1¹/₂'

2¹/₂" dia

³/₈"

1"

#10 bolt and washers
or copper rivet

3'

2¹/₂" dia

Taper to ³/₄" × 1"

8"

1" dia

³/₈" hole

Figure 56: Spar dimensions

Step G: Make the tiller.

1. The tiller is a single piece of mahogany or fir, 3 feet long. The after end is ³/₄ inch by 1¹/₄ inches, tapering to ³/₄ inch by ³/₄ inch at the forward end (see Figure 55). It is designed to be removed when not in use, which will help prevent damage.

2. Place the tiller in the rudderhead and allow it to protrude aft 1 inch. You will probably have to adjust the fit with a hand plane so it will be able to slide in and out easily. Mark the margins of the portion of the tiller in the rudderhead; this area is to be left square — the rest will be rounded off.

3. Shape two cheeks for the tiller, forward of the rudder, and glue them in place. I prefer to create an oval in cross section, but suit yourself.

4. Drill a ³/₈-inch hole in the after end of the tiller. To be sure the hole will be situated properly, put the tiller in the rudderhead and check that a pin through the hole will not bind and prevent the tiller from being raised or lowered.

5. Make a pin for the tiller, using a piece of ³/₈-inch dowel, 1³/₈ inch long. Sand the dowel until it will pass through the hole in the after end of the tiller without binding, and round off the ends. Drill ³/₁₆-inch holes, ³/₈ inch in from each end of the pin.

6. Whip with whipping line the end of a piece of ³/₁₆-inch line, 8 inches long, insert it in the hole in one end of the pin, and tie it off. Melt both ends of the line with a soldering iron to prevent unraveling, and form a point at the unwhipped end while it is still hot. Reinstall the tiller and put the pin in the hole. Pass the pointed end of the line through the other hole in the pin and tie it off with two half hitches.

Step H: Make the mast.
 Rounding the mast is much like rounding the oars, except the oars are oval along much of their length and the mast is a tapered round (see Figures 56, 57, and 58). As with the oars, you will first shape the mast stock to be four-sided, then eight-sided, then sixteen- sided, and then round.

81

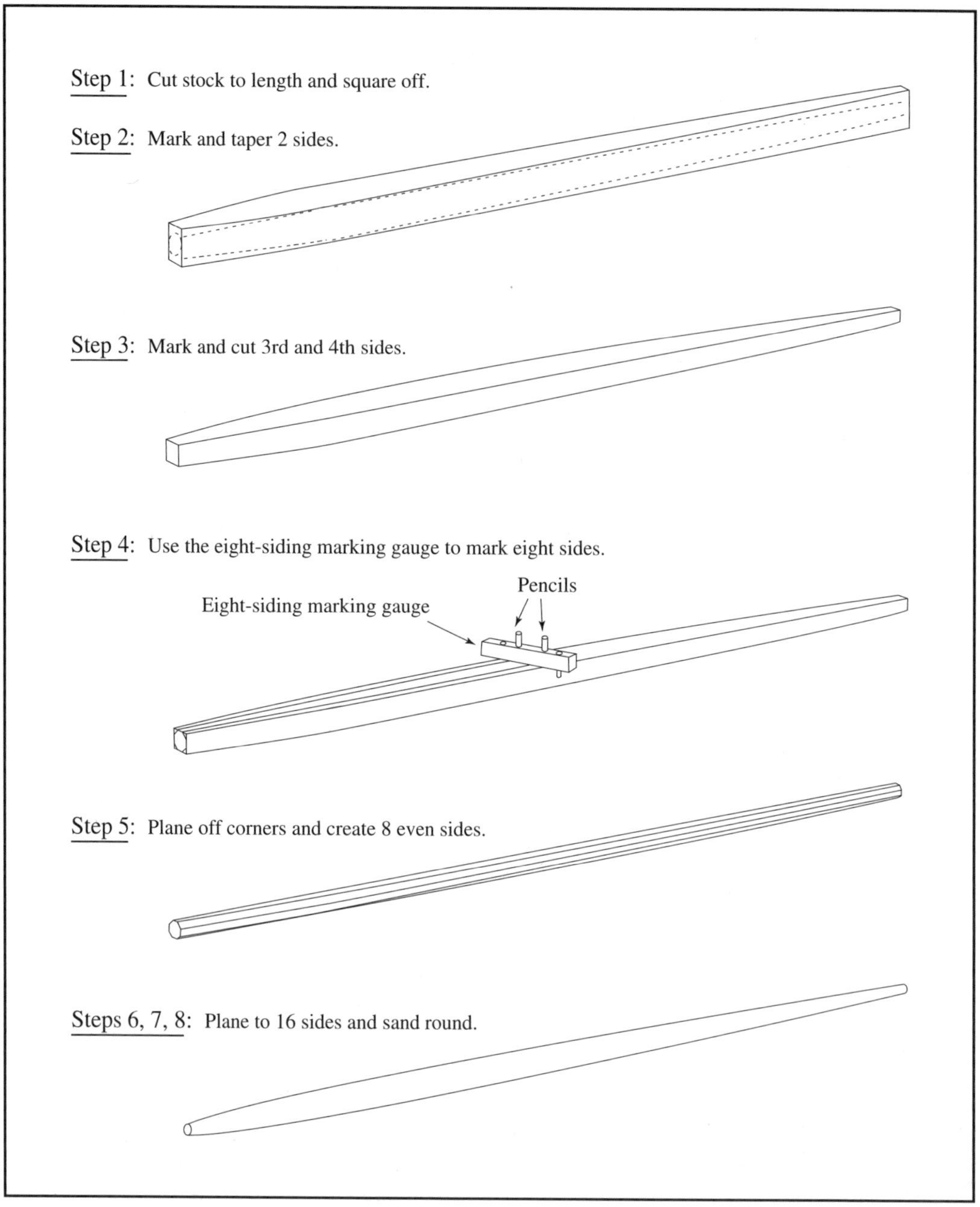

Figure 57: Shaping the mast

Step 1: Cut stock to length and square off.

Step 2: Mark and taper 2 sides.

Step 3: Mark and cut 3rd and 4th sides.

Step 4: Use the eight-siding marking gauge to mark eight sides.

Eight-siding marking gauge

Pencils

Step 5: Plane off corners and create 8 even sides.

Steps 6, 7, 8: Plane to 16 sides and sand round.

1. First square off an 11-foot length of spruce to 2½ inches. If you can't get the full thickness, glue up two pieces 1¼ inches thick or three pieces ⅞ inch thick.

2. To get to four sides, you first have to mark the shape on one side. Mark lines square across the stock at the locations shown in Figure 56. On the lines, mark the finished widths of the mast; center these on the stock. Spring your batten through the points; this will give you the taper on two sides of the mast. Cut to the outside of these lines, and plane fair.

3. Next, mark this same shape as above on a third side of the stock, and cut to the outside of the line. Plane these sides fair.

4. Mark the guidelines for planing the mast eight-sided (see Figure 57). To make the gauge, follow the drawing in Figure 58. To use the gauge, lay it on the mast blank, twisting it so the two dowels are pressed tightly against the sides. The dowels will follow the taper as you move the gauge; the narrower the width of the mast blank, the more diagonal to it the gauge becomes. As the gauge is moved down the blank, the pencils automatically mark the proper taper.

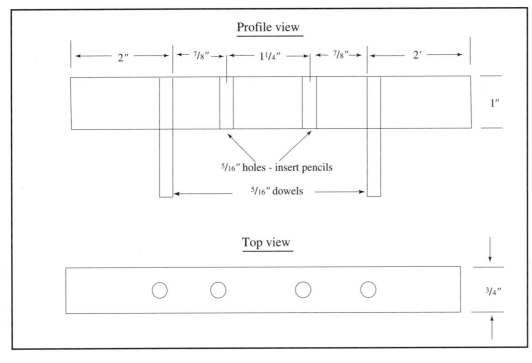

Figure 58: Making the eight-sided taper gauge

5. Plane off the four corners out to the guidelines. Take care that all eight sides are equal in width and that the taper of the mast is fair; there should be no noticeable humps or kinks.

6. Plane off the eight corners to create 16 sides of equal width.

7. Sharpen your block plane and set it for a fine cut. Plane off the sharp corners by taking long, overlapping strokes. Do not take a stroke in the same area twice in a row, and turn the mast as you go.

8. When you think the mast is as smooth as you can get it with the plane, fold a sheet of 60- or 80-grit sandpaper lengthwise and go over the mast, using the same stroking technique. When you can no longer feel sharp corners or lumps, switch to 100-grit, then 150.

9. Seal the mast with a sanding sealer; when dry, go over it with 220-grit sandpaper. Apply sealer again, and you are ready to varnish.

Step I: Make the sprit.

1. The sprit is made from a single piece of fir, ¾ inch by 1½ inches by 11 feet (see Figure 56). It is rectangular in section, tapering in both directions from 1½ inches at the center to 1 inch at the ends. Mark a line across the center (5½ feet from the ends); then mark 1-inch lines, centered, at the ends. Connect the ends of the lines with your batten and draw both sides of the taper. Then mark the locations for ⅜-inch holes at both ends; the inside edges of these holes are 1½ inches from the ends.

2. Round-over one end of the sprit as shown in Figure 56. Mark and cut a notch at the other end as shown.

3. Cut out the sprit. Smooth off the edges with your plane and round to ⅜ inch with your router or a plane.

4. Referring to the detail drawing in Figure 56, locate the holes for the #10 bolts, which act as reinforcements for the ends, and drill. If you wish, rivets can be used as substitutes for the bolts. A rivet consists of a copper nail driven through the drilled hole; a rove, or tightly fitting washer, is put over the protruding end of the nail, the nail is cut off slightly beyond the rove, and, while a bucking iron is held against the head of the nail, the end is peened over. Copper nails and roves to fit them can be purchased at most chandleries.

Fold a sheet of 100-grit sandpaper lengthwise and fair the sprit, then go to 150-grit. Seal, then sand with 220-grit, and reseal.

Step K: The sail

The sail can be made of Dacron or cotton (see Figure 47). Cotton sails, while rare these days, are still made. I have recommended a sailmaker, Nathaniel Wilson (see the resources section of Chapter 2), who knows how to build a cotton sail that will make the most hidebound traditionalist's heart sing. There are other folks who can do a fine job, too, so ask around.

Using a cotton sail is like maintaining a varnish finish. You have to be prepared to provide extra care, or it may mildew or otherwise be damaged. I leave the choice of weight and type of cotton sailcloth to the sailmaker. For a Dacron sail, I recommend a 4-ounce weight.

Step 1:
With Dacron waxed whipping line make a loop.

Step 2:
Wrap whipping around the line holding the loop
to the line. Leave tail showing.

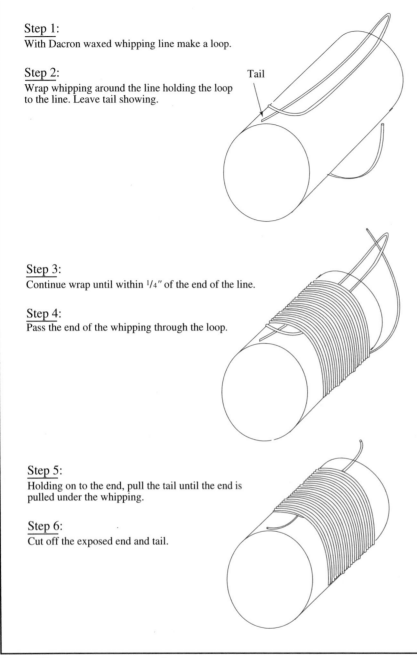

Tail

Step 3:
Continue wrap until within 1/4" of the end of the line.

Step 4:
Pass the end of the whipping through the loop.

Step 5:
Holding on to the end, pull the tail until the end is
pulled under the whipping.

Step 6:
Cut off the exposed end and tail.

Figure 59:
Whipping the end of the line

Step K: Rigging your boat (See Figure 47).

1. The sail is hoisted by a halyard of ¼-inch, 3-strand Dacron line passed through a ⅜-inch hole in the top of the mast. This is the simplest arrangement and works fine. If you prefer, tie on a small block (pulley) at the masthead. The halyard is tied off on the belaying pin. Remember that this pin also enables the halyard to hold the mast down, so don't leave it out.

2. The traveler is a length of ¼-inch, 3-strand Dacron line, the ends of which are passed through ¼-inch holes bored in the quarter knees.

3. The sheet is made of ⅜-inch, 3-strand Dacron line and is attached to the clew of the sail and passes through a ring on the traveler. It is tied off on one of two cleats, port and starboard.

4. When working with Dacron line, you should temporarily tape the cut ends so they don't unravel. Then use a match or a lighter to melt and fuse the ends. A proper whipping finishes the job (see Figure 59).

One easy way to cut and fuse Dacron ends in a single operation is with an electric soldering gun with a flat attachment made for cutting line. This automatically melts the ends as you cut.

5. To rig the daggerboard hold-down and adjuster (see Figure 46):

5a. Drill two ¼-inch holes on each side of the daggerboard trunk cap. These holes should line up with the center of the slot.

5b. Pass a 1-foot length of bungee cord through the holes and tie a figure-eight knot in one end. Melt the ends and whip them.

5c. Place the daggerboard in the trunk.

5d. Pull the bungee over the daggerboard and through the hole in the cap on the other side. Pull the cord until it tightens over the top of the daggerboard, then tie a stop knot. The bungee cord should be tight enough to keep the board from floating up, but it should be slack enough so you can push the cord over the end of the board and lift the board out. The bungee is properly tensioned when you are able to lift the board partway out of the trunk while the bungee still holds it in place.

XII

A Few Final Comments and Then We Launch Her

Well, here she is, your first boat. The challenge has been met; success is in your grasp. You have spent hours building the boat and watching it take shape, and now your great anticipation is launching day. There is, however, one more obstacle to overcome. The boat has to take up.

What's that, you say?

Taking up is the process of allowing the boat to soak up water, which will tighten the seams and make the hull watertight. If you planked the bottom with plywood, taking up is less critical than it is with a cross-planked bottom; only the seam at the chine, where the bottom meets the garboard plank, will have to take up. A cross-planked bottom, with all those seams, is another story.

The best way to allow the boat to take up is to put it in the water, fill it, and leave it immersed for anywhere from three to fourteen days, depending on how dry the planking is. Three or four days are usually enough. But most people are impatient for the official launching ceremony, so here are a few things that can be done to hasten taking up:

1. Put the boat on a waterproof tarp laid on the ground. Pull up the edges of the tarp and tie them off at the sheer. Fill the bottom with water up to 4 inches deep. Do not fill it to the rail. The boat is not designed to hold two tons of water! Allow the boat to sit for a few days, then untie the tarp. If it holds water, the seams have taken up.

Most boats will do fine with this treatment after a few days. Even if the seams seep a little when you launch her, it's no big deal. Wiggle your toes in the water, it feels great!

2. An alternative procedure is the same as the above, but begin by carefully pouring hot water along the seams, a little bit at a time. Do not use boiling water or pour huge amounts at one time, as the planks could cup, making the taking-up process more difficult. Don't be impatient. Use a little hot water, then follow the directions in Step 1, above. Leave the boat in the sun. Warm water works faster.

O.K., I'm turning you loose. Now go have fun with your new boat!